Reveal and Conceal

Contemporary Issues in the Middle East

An older woman from Upper Egypt meets with two young women who were born in Cairo. The younger of the two wears her everyday dress in public. The other is more modestly clad in a black overdress. The older woman covers her hair and neck more completely and opaquely. The child is dressed in the unisex outfit of the very young.

Reveal and Conceal

Dress in Contemporary Egypt

". . . And God has knowledge of what ye reveal and what ye conceal."
—Koran S 24:29

ANDREA B. RUGH

SYRACUSE UNIVERSITY PRESS   1986

Line drawings by Elizabeth Rodenbeck
Photographs by William A. Rugh

The paper used in this publication meets the minimum requirements of American National Standard for Information Sciences—Permanence of Paper for Printed Library Materials, ANSI Z39.48-1984. ∞™

Library of Congress Cataloging-in-Publication Data

Rugh, Andrea B.
    Reveal and conceal.

    (Contemporary issues in the Middle East)
    Bibliography: p.
    Includes index.
    1. Costume—Egypt. 2. Clothing and dress—Case studies. I. Title. II. Series.
GT1585.R84 1986   391'.00962   86-5889
ISBN 0-8156-2368-2 (alk. paper)

Manufactured in the United States of America

Contents

ANDREA B. RUGH received her Ph.D. from American University. Now an independent researcher and consultant, she has lived and worked in the Middle East for seventeen years. She is the author of *Coping with Poverty in a Cairo Community, Family in Contemporary Egypt,* and a number of articles on Egyptian family life. She is presently engaged in research on the socialization of children in a Syrian village.

Preface

CONTEMPORARY EGYPTIAN DRESS first began to interest me between 1976 and 1981, while I was conducting research in a lower-class urban quarter of Cairo. Over the previous several decades, the quarter attracted migrants from rural areas all over Egypt seeking "bread" or "to live" (the words are interchangeable in Egyptian colloquial Arabic). The migrants of different origins lived next door to one another, often one family per room in three- or four-story tenement houses that had seen better days during the period of Mohammad Ali, more than one hundred years before.

It was not long before I discovered the considerable sum of information the *baladi* (native folk) women glean from a chance meeting with a stranger in the quarter, even when their conversation is cursory and contains little overt information. When they meet, the women subject each other to a scrutiny that filters through details of dress, manner, speech, and gesture to find clues that place the other in known and understood categories. So unconscious is the process that only a direct question brings out the evaluation of the appraiser, who might say, in an off-hand way, "Well, she comes from an area west of Assyut in Upper Egypt, is a Christian and poor, and has not lived very long in Cairo." As a useful exercise, I tried to learn the details that would make me capable of drawing similar kinds of conclusions. But so abundant was the detail from their varied origins in the dress and manner of these inhabitants that I quickly abandoned the task as impossible in that setting.

A complicating factor was that so many details relied for their meaning on their particular context:

> "How do you know that woman is a Christian?" I would ask. "Because she is wearing a black shawl of the kind many Christians wear," was my companion's answer. On another occasion I would comment, "The woman in the store buying material was a Christian wasn't she, because she wore the black shawl?" "No, she was an *Arab* (bedouin), because of the way she spoke and because she was asking about bedouin material to make the dresses they wear." "But

why then do you assume that most women who wear shawls are Christians?" "Because in this quarter the majority of the people are Muslims who come from the provinces of the Delta where the shawl is not so commonly worn. Women here who wear the shawl usually come from Upper Egypt, and those from Upper Egypt who live in the quarter frequently come from the areas which are Christian or they would be wearing Nubian dress or the dress of Muslim farmers south of the Christian areas. If they were Muslims or Nubians from the south they would also probably be living in other quarters than this one, where their own kind tend to settle."

The meanings are subtle and deep, built on years of absorbing significant details. But significance is relative and bounded—reserved for the understanding of those to whom it matters. If I should ask an established middle-class or upper-class Egyptian to describe the details of baladi or *fellaha* (farmwoman) dress, more often than not they would say, "Oh they all wear the same old black dress with a *tarha* (long scarf) on their head." Only the most observant, or the ones with memories from childhood, remember the details of a favorite servant girl's dress, or what the vegetable peddler's wife wears.

In early 1980, I set out systematically to trace the patterns of dress throughout Egypt—unwinding, in effect, the tangled web of costumes from the Cairo quarter back to the single strands of their beginnings. The backbone of the study was accomplished in a four-week sail up the Nile, observing village by village the permutations of dress in Upper Egypt and, when mooring by the banks at evening, asking the necessary questions about dress. The Nile brings the population to its banks every day for water, to wash clothes, to bathe, to cross over to its other bank for marketing or visits, or simply to sit. In Upper Egypt it is the magnetic pole around which activity rotates. For me the Nile offered the opportunity to see women in their most informal garb by their door stoops, and in their most formal finery, piled in small sailing ferry boats on their way to market on the opposite bank.

I should mention that though it may appear an easy task to the reader to ask questions about dress, this is not the case in rural Egypt. To begin with, people find it difficult to take seriously a foreigner who asks questions about Egyptian folkdress. And secondly, personal questions of any kind are an invasion of privacy permitted to strangers only after passing at least a minimal amount of time getting acquainted. It is sometimes frustrating to see an interesting feature of dress whiz by as one sits in a car, late for an appointment or reluctant to subject companions to the lengthy small talk needed to lead up to questions about dress. The times I have cut short the small talk, the answers have been given unwillingly and in a perfunctory manner: "Oh this, it is a *futa*" (general rather than specific term for a modesty head cover). "And this detail, call it what you will. Everyone around here wears this style: old, young, this town, next town" (when in fact, those in the next town wear something different, and young women of the same village, something else). If the same questions are asked in the context of a broader conversation, however, the answers are often subtle and complicated, leading on to more important discoveries. Still, it is not always easy to discern facts from the fictions suggested by people because at some moment they don't feel like answering what seem to be trivial questions. I have returned many times to some areas to confirm answers that do not seem accurate. In the end therefore it is quite possible that despite all my attempts to prevent them, errors still exist because of these difficulties. If so, I take full responsibility for not having pursued a fact as diligently as I should.

By train and by car I travelled Upper and Lower Egypt forward and back on roadbeds and highways that paralleled the Nile a few kilometers inland. I made extended visits to provincial towns of Upper Egypt, the southern oases, and Fayoum, crisscrossed the more complicated Delta area, and followed along much of the Northern coast. When the Sinai was returned to Egypt I took two trips, one to the northern settlements and one to the south, to the areas around St. Catherine's monastery. Since 1982 I have also returned to Egypt each year in a continuing study of Upper and Lower Egyptian villages that has allowed me a deeper and more penetrating view of dress in the specific locations of these villages.

The book that results from these travels has limited objectives. It is not an attempt to catalogue Egyptian traditional costume in minute detail, either as it exists now or existed in the past. This task is presently being ably carried out by an Egyptian, Shahira Mehrez, who is in far better position to trace the origin of changes in terminology and detail. The present book, instead, seeks significance in contemporary dress to discover the meaningful categories, conscious and unconscious, that underlie its clusters of features, and to learn more about the inherent features in the dynamics of dress that set up self-limiting constraints on its usage.

At times the quest has led to exciting discoveries, as when relationships appear between costumes that suggest the sources of people's identities. There is, for example, the Upper Egyptian dress called *Shargawi* which comes from the Delta, or the Harrah oasis dress with its details from the Nile Valley, or the influences carried deep in the countryside in the Delta, to Fayoum or to the oases of the Western desert along caravan routes and waterways. There are many such traces of the past, where people are no longer conscious of the original inspiration. In such examples it is sometimes only possible to mention apparent connections and leave to later historians the task of unravelling the sequence of their appearance. Such is the case with the Upper Egyptian *tawb,* a museum-piece Nubian embroidered dress, and dresses of the four oases of the Kharga complex. Discoveries like these are the rewards of becoming a dress-watcher. They have surprised me with the amount of present and past that is stamped indelibly for

all to see on the every-day costumes of folk Egyptians. It is only necessary to edu-
cate the eye to discover these subtle traces.

From the beginnings of ethnography, in its most incipient forms, ethnog-
raphers have felt the need to describe the dress of "natives," as if in the description the true nature of the difference between West and East might appear. In
folkloric museums around the world, costumes are validly preserved as art forms,
historic analogues, or simple reference points. But an important dimension is
often overlooked by not viewing the costumes of a culture in relation to one another with their customary permutations and grand patternings. It is through
such comparisons of what is stable and fleeting in dress that we develop a deeper
understanding of what Egyptians view as the socially meaningful categories of
their lives.

This preface would not be complete without acknowledging some of the
people who shared the pursuit of dress styles by design or by happenstance.
There are Mary and Henry Horsey who were my companions on the Nile trip,
and Ramadan, our boatman, who knows the river and its people intimately. There
is my long-time friend, Ansaf Aziz, whose knowledge of the urban folk classes
makes communication with them easy. Her whole-hearted support for any project I attempt always strengthens my resolve to be worthy of such faithfulness.
Her mother, in frustration over trying to describe the old two-piece *hubbara* to
me, sat down and made one on the sewing machine for me. Mary Megelli, the
indefatigable traveller, accompanied me on several trips to fill in gaps, and still
diligently reports interesting details from her own trips around Egypt. Jane Ali
Hassan spent an unforgettable week camping with me in Bahriya oasis and visiting oasis women, including the famous seamstress Sitt Anoona in the village of
Agouz. My colleague in a continuing study of Egyptian education, Wade Robin-
son, also deserves recognition for his patience with the details of dress that frequently distract me from total concentration on our project. By now he is as
well versed in the features of Egyptian dress as I am. Another friend, Nayra Atiya,
is responsible, at least in part, for helping me develop a warm and deep feeling
for Egypt and its people.

I want to thank also Riaya Nimr and her husband, Abu Aineen, who permitted me to photograph their collection of folk dresses. Both are devoted to
the preservation of Egyptian traditional arts. So, too, is Shahira Mehrez, who was
so willing to share with me the knowledge she has painstakingly gathered around
Egypt, especially with regard to Delta dresses. Her expertise has been recognized
in dress exhibitions both in Cairo and the United States. I especially feel grate-
ful for her assistance.

Two others helped me in the collection of proverbs, my elderly friend, Mme.

Habib Said, who revels in an intellectual task of this kind, and the scholarly re-tired teacher, Hezkial Bastaurous, whom Mme. Habib sent me to see in Assyut. His must be the most complete unpublished collection of Arabic proverbs found anywhere in the world.

Another special thanks goes to Elizabeth Rodenbeck, who so sympatheti-cally drew the black and white sketches that accompany the text. Her long-term residence in Egypt and sympathy for its people give her a keen eye for the de-tails of people's lives.

My final thanks go to my family, William, David, Douglas, and Nicholas, who as in my other studies of Egypt, deserve recognition for their patience and forbearance with my single-minded enthusiasms. Doug is to be especially thanked for typing most of the manuscript, Nick for typing the revisions, and William for participating in several of my trips, taking most of my photographs of dress, and tracking down many details with as much enthusiasm as I.

To all these people goes my gratitude for what they have contributed to this book and, more important, my gratitude for their friendship which makes re-turning to Egypt always such a warm and comforting event.

The research for much of this study was carried out in the middle to late 1970s. At that time the Egyptian pound was worth about $1.40. Now in the 1980s the value of the dollar is considerably higher, and, with a rampant inflation, so are prices. As of January 1986, at the official rate, the Egyptian pound is worth U.S. $.75. A sewing machine that in 1978 cost about £E 30 now costs more than £E 100. Unless otherwise specified, prices quoted in the text are 1970s prices. Readers should keep in mind that prices are much higher now.

Reveal and Conceal

Reveal and Conceal

"Eat what you like; dress to please others"[1] — Arab proverb

THE RHYTHMS of human social life follow patterns often discernible without being fully predictable. Once one stumbles on evidence of a dearly held value, one finds it like an echo in other facets of the daily life of a people. Dress is only one in a number of entry points into the conceptual life of a society.

Dress patterns are as much a symbolic language as the verbal structures anthropologists attend to so closely. Like languages, they have an internalized transformational grammar that sets the rules for conveying meaning and provides the keys for discerning their implications. Dress patterns provide one convenient way to study a social order, and the social principles that organize it, that has all too often been overlooked in the past.

It was Kroeber who was the first in 1919, in an article appearing in the *American Anthropologist* (21:235–63) entitled, "On the Principle of Order in Civilization as Exemplified by Changes of Fashion," to point out how an examination of formal dress fashions (seen over the period 1844 to 1919) could illuminate unconscious supra-individual tendencies in society. This first essay, he later noted, showed "no more than that there are stylistic trends of an amplitude, effectiveness and duration indicating that they are governed by factors unknown but which must be superindividual" (Richardson and Kroeber 1940:152).

In 1940, with Richardson, he expanded the first study to a survey of three hundred years of dress fashion; after completing this, he felt even more strongly convinced that some cultural patterns lead an independent life of their own, separate from the designs of prominent trend-setters in an historic period. Individuals acted only as agents of tendencies over which they had no independent influence.

Richardson and Kroeber drew these conclusions from the examination over time of the fluctuations in six dimensions of dress: the lengths and widths of skirt, waist, and decolletage. Despite annual and other short-term fluctuations,

---

1. One Egyptian's interpretation of this proverb was: It is not important what you eat, but what you wear shows others who you are.

an overall pattern of oscillation between extremes of these dimensions[2] appeared so regular as to preclude the unique effects of special events for particular people. As each dimension moves further from a particular ideal pattern,[3] they said, the probability increases that it will reverse its direction and move back toward the ideal. In normal periods, dress remains fairly standard in its basic proportions. But in periods of sociocultural stress, variability increases considerably, not as a direct result of the stress, but rather because it "disrupt[s] the established dress style and tend[s] to its overthrow or inversion" (Richardson and Kroeber 1940:149).

The essential element in the Richardson and Kroeber study was their notion that a stable ideal dress pattern existed around which fluctuations in dimension could be measured. Any fashions of the moment that differed from the ideal were fleeting and unsubstantial when compared with the ideal pattern's permanence and stability as the measure of centrality.

In a much later paper Marvin Harris criticized the rigidity of this ideal pattern concept and the fixed limits of fluctuation that Richardson and Kroeber imposed. Harris quotes Richardson and Kroeber as saying that "the upper limits of possibility, and probably our less defineable limits of decency" had been reached in 1927 when the skirt arrived at the knee (Harris 1973:22). For Harris, with the advantage of hindsight, the fact that the skirt eventually surged over the knee caused "the basic pattern (to oscillate) itself right out of existence" (Harris 1973: 22). Otherwise Harris agreed with Richardson and Kroeber that it is large-scale cultural forces rather than individuals who control fashion swings.

Kroeber's theories of supra-individual forces have long since been discredited as unnecessarily vague and lacking in explanatory power, but no one to date has attempted to develop an understanding in another framework of the periodicities he discovered, or sought to test his theories of oscillations in other areas of the world or in other dimensions of dress. My desire to shed light on issues raised by Kroeber is one incentive for this study.

Dress patterns are intriguing from other angles, too. There is more to dress than grand design, just as there is more to dress than the simple sheltering from the elements. As a symbolic language, dress reveals some of the conscious and unconscious priorities people hold. Normally, although a person is not compelled to wear a particular fashion, choice is so circumscribed by normative prescriptions, sanctioned inducements, conventions, and socially cherished values that for any individual there may, in fact, be little latitude in what clothing he or she finally adopts. This is especially true when restrictions of availability and re-

2. A complete cycle from one extreme dimension to its opposite and back took approximately 100 years.

3. "This basic or ideal pattern (in formal dress) for Europe of the last two or three centuries requires a skirt that is both full and long, a waist that is abnormally constricted but in nearly proper anatomical position, and decolletage that is ample both vertically and horizontally" (Richardson and Kroeber 1940:149).

source are added to the equation. Dress is thus at one and the same time both the outcome of collective thinking and a flexible medium people manipulate to project the kind of public image they want others to know them by.

The outside observer may never know for sure what are intentional, unknowing, or accidental arrangements in dress elements. To some degree the reasons why a wearer chooses to reveal or conceal aspects of the physical or psychological self will always remain shrouded from outsiders. Part of the excitement of dress resides in the uncertainty whether, for example, an overly exposed piece of flesh is an inadvertent or a provocative act. Conventions in dress, by providing common reference points, permit people to communicate unambiguous meanings when they so desire or, just as equally, to obscure meanings that are not intended for public consumption. Nevertheless the outsider can come to know the range of a society's choices and discover the general meanings assigned to dress elements in a particular cultural setting.

Arrangements of significant elements in dress, like arrangements in other human symbolic systems, are subject to the constraints of human thought processes. Human beings tend to set up differences as symbolic oppositions and the outer limits between which elements vary, as bipolar extremes. There is both a static and a fluid quality to these oppositions. On the one hand there are fairly stable understandings for what is long or short, wide or narrow, light or dark, decorated or undecorated. On the other hand, dress styles may occupy a place along the continuum between the extremes according to momentary definitions of what is modest or immodest, form-concealing or form-revealing, appropriate or inappropriate, garish or in good taste.

Tension between the extremes — the fact that one is meaningful only in relation to the other — builds a whole that allows not only room for variability but seeks a satisfactory reconciliation for its warring parts at any given moment. Judgements of what is "just right" serve to buttress the reconciliations. While extremes of shape and cut are vaguely constrained by the anatomy of human shape, moral dimensions compose a sliding scale that varies over social space and time. What it is to be a "nice girl" now may remain in final essentials much the same as it was two decades ago but circumstances now require that these essentials be preserved by entirely new behaviors. The Egyptian university student preserves her "niceness" in ways quite different from her grandmother who rarely left the confines of the family garden except, as the saying goes, when born, married, or dead.

There are no neat oscillations from, say, nakedness to shrouding and back again, that can be successfully constrained to regular time periods, as Kroeber reported. Rather, in Egypt, styles and dress dimensions vary across time and physical space in irregular intervals even while in regular progression from one extreme dimension to the other. The dialectic of extreme dimensions assures that each carries inherent in it the seeds of its own demise. As styles move precariously closer toward one extreme, the greater grows the attractiveness to trend setters to turn back to centrist or contrasting styles. The longer the extreme style has lasted historically, or the more widely it is distributed, the greater is the impact of yet another change in style.

The sweep of fluctuation slows under certain conditions, firming oppositions into persistent contrasting styles that exist side by side. The most common example of this occurs when two styles become identified as markers of antagonistic social groups. Then it becomes difficult for individuals of one group to assume the markers of the other without also demonstrating a willingness for rapprochement. Fluctuations also slow when a particular dress style or element is deemed so satisfactory in a particular context that change would only serve to reduce the advantages. We will see examples of all these kinds of dress in the text.

What is conceived of here, then, is already different from Kroeber with his "core ideal pattern" of dress around which individual patterns fluctuate. Here the problem is seen as one of opposites whose counteracting attractions set up tensions which lead to moderation, while still retaining the magnetism of their own polarities.

The most inclusive opposition in dress is the polarity of revelation and concealment in both physical and psychological senses. People are not likely to find simple answers when they make decisions about what to wear and how to wear it. The rural woman, for example, even with choice of style severely limited, may ask herself, "Can I attract the attentions of a mate more readily with modest, concealing clothing or by clothing that displays my feminine charms?" Or she may worry whether the display of wealth in her clothing will attract the evil eye. She may wonder whether to identify her origins by known markers in an unfamiliar place, reaping both the rewards and disadvantages of those affiliations, or to walk anonymously among strangers, saving the more subtle signs she wishes to communicate to members of the inner circle. Her answers to these questions may cause her to wear clothes that differ markedly in detail in either case.

Why study Egypt and why the emphasis on women's folk dress? Most important in both cases is the variety that exists in these subjects. Egypt's position at a geographical crossroads gives to its dress indigenous and introduced styles, sometimes from far-away origins. Also, several of its population subgroups share elements of dress with peoples living contiguous to the political boundaries of the national state. Add to this a restricted resource base that for centuries has made the choice of folk dress style a deliberate and generally conservative act. Such standard conventional forms of dress develop subtle nuances that convey meanings to specified audiences. Dress reinforces social boundaries by distinguishing between those who attend to the specified meanings and those who do not.

In Egypt these distinctions are all-important. Gross class and other socioeconomic characteristics are easier to identify by similarities of dress than by any corresponding distinctions of income, occupation, or educational level. Women's dress in particular has preserved the widest range of subtle markers and consequently yields much greater descriptive information. Men have reduced to a handful the distinctions that are now important in their dress. In short, Egypt offers the opportunity to observe dress in a rich and elaborated tradition that blends new with old, indigenous with foreign, in a context where as yet the homogenization of contemporary society has not fully blurred the cogency of difference.

As anthropologists we are constantly on the lookout for ways to identify indigenous categories—to find how people of a culture sort through the elements of their environment and compartmentalize their conceptions into meaningful units. One task of this book is to examine the extent to which dress provides a code which can decipher the complexities of social structures and the values on which they are based. It is important also to examine the possibilities extant in dress codes to act as barometers of change in social life. Do people signal their new allegiances in the visible signs of dress, or do conventions so hinder rapid readjustment that dress only serves as a record of what is stable or past in social history?

This book is organized into four major sections. The first, which is introductory, includes this chapter which describes the conceptual rationale for the work, and the second chapter which outlines the general types of dress in Egypt and their basic elements. The second section, Chapters 2 through 5, catalogs the geographical and community understandings that are delineated by dress. These constitute the broad sets of dress conventions within which individuals must make their choices of dress. Chapters 6 and 7 constitute the third section where individuals are shown manipulating elements of personal identity and status in their dress. Finally, the last chapter provides both summary and conclusion by examining the dialectic of dress symbols in Egypt across space and time.

The book, like the symbols of dress it portrays, is intended to show several layers of significance. The title, *Reveal and Conceal*, suggests this broader agenda. On one level, dress reveals clues to the outsider of what is meaningful in Egyptian society. On the other, it conceals what should be kept inviolable in the private details of family life and procreation. At the community level, dress symbolizes a pride in ethnic community, locale, and honor, but hides the mundane everyday details that interfere with the presentation of that pride. At the individual level, complicated inventories of dress elements and modes of artfully displaying them give plenty of room for concealing or revealing the psychological and physical dimensions of the self. Finally, in the grand design of dress style distribution across time and space (which no one but the determined analyst recognizes) comes clear something of the inherent nature of the symbolic processes in human thought.

The book in certain ways follows the research process. It allows the patterns to emerge as they are observed in gross details first and then narrows to the finer details that only become understood with time. Around these observations is then woven the context that comes from the wearers' comments and other related observations. In this book it is dress that should speak out on indigenous categories, and only after it has spoken do we look at other sources to confirm the truth of its assertions.

One final note: this study is concerned with developing an understanding of the way social symbols are used, and stresses the elements in dress that are normally visible to the eye—what is immediately or potentially observable—for only those elements convey social messages to a broad audience.

Folk Dress

"A tailor's fee is always in his hand"—Arab proverb

EGYPTIAN DRESS can be roughly divided in two major subdivisions: that worn by the masses of the "traditional" social classes, both rural and urban, and that worn by the educated, mostly urban, classes. The first is a distinctively native Egyptian dress and the second corresponds in general features with international styles. One way to distinguish these two styles is to call them "traditional" and "modern," which in essence is how many Egyptians think of them. To make such easy distinctions, however, glosses over the fact that both are contemporary styles and both include many features that are continuously in the process of change. Both also follow certain conventions that have existed for long periods of time in Egyptian society. Using terms like "traditional" and "modern" therefore has the disadvantage of seeming to be co-opted by those Egyptian classes which view modern as good and traditional as inferior. For this reason it seems more appropriate to distinguish the styles with the terms "folk" (baladi, fellahi, *shab'i*), including the mass of the Egyptian urban and rural lower social classes, and "foreign" (*frangi*), the term used by Egyptians to designate "modern" dress of foreign inspiration. This book deals mainly with folk styles which tend to have a wide variety of subtle meanings that are less well understood, but foreign dress and other middle class styles are dealt with briefly in Chapter 6.

FOLK STYLES

Female Folk Dress

Egyptian female folk dress consists of three major elements: a basic dress, an outer modesty garment and a head covering (see Chapters 3 and 4 for details). The dress is one that maximally covers the body and head, leaving only the face, hands, ankles, and sometimes the feet uncovered. The garments are generally commodious but not unattractive. Considerable skill is exercised in the use of artful tucks and draping materials to shape the figure to good effect.

The average peasant, urban lower-class, or bedouin woman does not have a large wardrobe. She is limited in the first instance by her resources, which seldom allow for extravagance in clothing. She may have no more than one or two new dresses made a year, bought usually at the time of the two Muslim feasts which mark the end of the Ramadan fasting month and the yearly pilgrimage period. She tends to choose her clothing conservatively so that this year's best dress (*fustan*) can serve as next year's second best (*galabiya,* a general term for dress) and the third year's work dress. Dresses are thus not ordinarily acquired for separate purposes; the same style can serve all purposes and often only differs in whether it is old or new. It is usually considered a sign of affluence to buy specific clothes for specific occasions. For this reason folk dress tends to remain stable over much longer periods of time than the dress of urban elites, which seeks variety and novelty and is designed for the specialized occasions of sport, parties, office, and everyday.

Evidence in Lane (1954 org. 1860) shows that the elites of today have retained little of what was fashionable in nineteenth-century styles. However, a few items of elite dress (primarily modesty cloaks) have been adopted by today's lower classes, who, at the same time, have not diverged far from what was already a basic style for them in the nineteenth century. Stability in this case implies a stability of certain limits that the folk classes observe, even while experimenting in a restrained way with the dimensions and details of dress. By contrast, the elites' desire for variety seems to allow them periodically to define wholly new sets of limits as they did during the era of the mini-skirt and as we shall see they are doing now with the new Islamic dress. Elite dress styles viewed at distinctly different points in time therefore bear little resemblance to one another, while those of the folk classes tend to bear a definite relationship.

One example of the persistence of a folk style most certainly imitated from the current elites is the style (see description under "Boheira" in Chapter 3) introduced by the women who accompanied Napoleon's forces at the turn of the eighteenth century. The present-day folk costume still recognizably follows the outlines of that style, modified to local modesty requirements but preserving the "immodest" decolletage in decorative piping.

Most items of folk apparel are made up for the individual from measures of cloth and, with the exception of some modesty garments, underclothes, stockings, and shoes, are not found ready-made. Men and women often buy materials from travelling peddlers who go door to door through villages and street by street through urban lower-class neighborhoods. Women earn income sometimes by buying bolts of material wholesale and selling to their neighbors at retail prices. Selection of materials by either of these methods is limited.

Any fair-sized town with a market is likely also to have a material salesman with his wares spread out on the ground. Villagers know well the cost and quality of most of his goods, forearming themselves before they buy with the latest price quotations from others who have made recent purchases. It is because the local scene offers so little variety and so little in the way of competitive prices that visits to commercial sections of bigger country towns and cities are popular. There, in material *souqs* (bazaars) with acres of small shops carrying bolts of material from floor to ceiling, the selection is expanded. Still the stores, obtaining their supplies from the same wholesalers, duplicate each other in kinds and patterns of Egyptian-made yard goods, and, increasingly, in foreign-made synthetics.

Men are often the purchasers of yard goods for themselves and their women. Only if transportation to nearby cities is convenient and cheap are women allowed to make regular trips to buy the necessities of the house, and then only in the company of their men or with groups of their female relatives.

The most popular and inexpensive materials for women's basic dresses in winter and summer are cottons. Lighter weights sell at a minimum of about 50p ($.70 in 1981) a meter but for better qualities are more likely to sell for about £E 1.00 ($1.40) a meter. Heavier weights for winter, called *kustor,* sell at a government subsidized and rationed price of 16p or 20p ($0.22 or $0.28) a meter and a general rate of about 50p or more. Kustor at its best is a well-made, strong cotton that is a recognized bargain by lower-class women. As is the case for many locally made fabrics, flaws in design patterns and weave are common, necessitating a close scrutiny of the cloth before it is purchased. The Egyptian customer tolerates flaws in inexpensive Egyptian materials partly because he or she has little choice. One consequence of this tolerance is the conviction of the superiority in quality of foreign over locally made goods. Less frequently, dresses are also made from more expensive materials: velvet, silk, satin, "smoking" (a corded rayon blend material that costs several pounds a meter), synthetics and, recently, polyester knits.

Dresses are made in the household of the wearer herself, a neighbor, or a local seamstress. In some villages, men are the specialists who sew for men and women. Sewing is a skill that women are anxious to acquire if only for its usefulness in outfitting their own families. Numerous opportunities exist in government social centers, school programs, and private charities for girls to learn sewing, and women who sew well are assured a steady source of income in a village. The proverb "A tailor's fee is always in his hand," expresses the advantages of sewing as a profession where because of the material at hand, the fee cannot be refused.

For each dress, seamstresses earn 35 to 50p and sometimes more for elaborate dresses or when sewing for more affluent clients; costs tend to equal what the traffic can bear.[1] However, for the lower-class household, steady work by the

---

1. Urban tailors and seamstresses sewing for middle and upper class clients earn up to £E 10 or £E 25 for a dress or woman's suit.

women dishonors the men as unable to support their families. As a result, full-time seamstresses tend to be unmarried or widowed women whose circumstances justify their need for work. To sew without fee for family and friends, however, is to share a valuable skill that will be reciprocated by gifts and services at some other time.

The skill of seamstresses varies. Many put together the most basic models in a slipshod way that is immediately apparent to the casual observer. Others are highly skilled in the most intricate patterns. To set up business a seamstress needs a machine. The most common table-top hand-crank model costs £E 30 or about $42. For an additional amount a motor can be attached when electricity is available.

The material required for the usual full-length folk dress with long sleeves, of the common 80 to 90 cm (about one yard) wide (*ard*) local yard goods, is 4½ to 5 meters. Foreign materials usually come in the *ard w nuss* width of about 45 inches (115 cm) which of course requires less. The dressmaker converts the measurements of her client into the *shibr* (about 20 cm) or the width between the tip of her finger and thumb when the fingers are extended as far as possible. Two other measures are used less frequently and usually are not named. These are the measures between the right shoulder bone and the extended right thumb (about 75 cm), and between the left shoulder bone and the right thumb (about one meter). In some parts of the Middle East these are called *idraa'* and *idraa' w sidra* respectively. Some women use the standard floor tile as a measure, when a house affords such amenities. Four tiles equal a meter. (See Chapter 5 for more on standard cloth measures.)

Since she is always her own measure, the seamstress standardizes the length of dimensions she uses for her calculations on her customers. For the length of sleeves and skirts, she may simply use the material itself as a measuring tape, making suitable allowances for hems and seams. She measures and then cuts and rips until she has the basic parts of the dress. Only minimal amounts are cut away at neck and under the arm, or in narrowing the waist to conform with the contours of the body. Tucks are common but darts are less so. Fullness is reduced by tucks and increased by gathers.

Many seamstresses make a single standard model. A more skilled one may have a standard style with a range of decorative variations from which the customer can choose. The seams are sometimes covered with braid, lace, or other decorative cording, either in the same color as the dress or contrasting with it. Tucks around the sleeve or close to the lower hem of a dress make it possible to adjust the material to the wearer's dimensions either when new or after the material has shrunk with several washings. Tucks however are not wholly functional; many are considered a vital part of the decorative design.

The second component of folk dress, the modesty garment, has a variety of forms that range from an outer dress in the same style as the underneath, basic

Granny style of Lower
Egypt: neckline variation.

dress, to a variety of kinds of cloaks and shawls that either envelop or only cover the form partially (see Chapter 3 for more details). When the modesty covering is a dress, it is made up in the manner described above for the basic dress. In all cases it is black in color and its material in the city is likely to be a silky or shiny material like silk, rayon, or satin; in the country it will be made of a heavy cotton or wool; among some groups, it may even be an almost transparent net material.

Other modesty coverings of certain common types like shawls are bought ready-made in rayon or silk weaves, or in velvets, all with elaborately knotted fringes of macrame. The art of macrame originated in the Middle East to serve this purpose of controlling the loose ends of woven materials on shawls and head coverings.

Other less common varieties of modesty covering such as the large red and black woven rectangle of Bahriya oasis or the yellow and black checked cloth of parts of Upper Egypt are also bought ready-made. Now women usually buy ready-made short head scarves in colored prints from bazaar stalls where they flutter in profusion.

Any remaining types of head coverings and modesty garments are usually bought as material by the meter and finished into veils cloaks, and scarves (with crocheted, beaded, or tufted tassels as edging). Store keepers set aside a variety of grades of material made especially for these purposes. The cheapest forms of materials for these purposes are *shash,* a kind of semi-transparent to opaque muslin of loose weave that is used for head veils and outer modesty dresses. More expensive garments are of rayon, silk, or silk blends, but range also through a variety of cotton weights as well. A tarha head veil which requires 2½ or 3 meters of chiffon or crepe georgette may cost about 9 £E ($12.60). In some areas of the country wools of various degrees of coarseness are woven at home or by specialists and used as large shawls for modesty coverings.

Observers often comment on how dysfunctional Egyptian women's folk dress appears to be with its voluminous layers of material that seem to interfere with mobility, and its extensive use of the color black that absorbs the hot rays of the Egyptian sun. Human dress in most countries, even those unable to afford extensive use of artificially cooled environments, has departed considerably from what is strictly utilitarian in terms of climatic conditions. However in Egypt, dress is still reasonably suitable to both the climate and the activities of the people. Generous skirts provide a requisite amount of modesty in the squatting position women assume for many of their activities. Picked up a layer at a time, skirts and modesty garments are useful carrying vehicles for fodder, market purchases, and sometimes even babies. They catch the stray bits of rice or vegetable in food preparation and protect the legs against scratches in field work. Dark outer garments and head scarves protect the inner clothes from the dirt and dust of village streets and in the case of head scarves protect against the spread of lice from one person to another. Amply scooped bosoms or side slits allow women to lift out one breast at a time for nursing babies.

A recent study reported in *Nature* magazine questions the assumption that black or dark clothing makes its wearer more uncomfortable than lighter clothing. According to the study, although black garments absorb more than 2½ times as much radiation as white garments (making the temperature at the surface of black garments five degrees hotter) the additional heat is lost on the inner side of the garment before it reaches the wearer's body. This process is aided by the flowing nature of the dress that sets up the convection currents of a natural air conditioning system.

So, even though dress in the Egyptian context is not strictly devised on the basis of utilitarian principles, it is convenient enough so that changes in style are not precipitated on grounds of inconvenience alone.

Male Folk Dress

Egyptian male folk dress has two components which vary with enough consistency to reveal clues of important identities. These are the basic robe (galabiya) and the head covering. From accounts in Lane, it appears that in the nineteenth century men's dress had a much more complicated set of markers for identifying sub-groups of Egyptian society. Though the robes of both poorer and higher classes were basically similar—long, flowing gowns with wide sleeves, much like those worn today by the folk classes—similarities ceased when it came to the elaboration of details, the fineness of workmanship and materials, and the number of formal outer garments. The lower classes wore drawers, a long shirt-like garment, and over that in cold weather an *abaya* (cloak). Men of the higher classes wore the drawers and the shirt, and over them a short vest (*sidari*), and then a *kuftan* (robe). The wide sleeves of the kuftan were cut to above the wrists exposing the hands; but in the presence of someone of higher rank the sleeves were arranged to cover the hands. Over the kuftan was worn a *jubba* (over-robe), and over that or replacing it was the ceremonial robe, the *benish*. Another similar over-robe called the *faragiya* was chiefly worn by men of the learned professions. Some men of the middle classes concealed their finery when going out by wearing a black cotton robe similar to that of the lower classes. Added to the many-layered outfits of these classes were shawls, sashes, and a whole range of colorful head coverings, including a black woolen cloak or abaya like that of the lower class but of finer quality (Lane 1954 orig. 1860:30–34).

The turban was also more elaborated than it is in most places now in Egypt. It consisted of a small, cotton cap, covered with a *tarboosh*[2] and wrapped with a headcloth. The color of this last cloth had some significance in identifying class and religious groups, as, for example, a green scarf which signified a descendant of the Prophet (see Chapter 7 for more distinctions). Lane notes that servants wore the most formal turbans. Men of religion also wore wide and formal turbans called *mukla* (Lane 1954 orig. 1860:34–36).

In Egypt today (with the exception of religious sheikhs, who still retain a dress of office similar in certain aspects to the dress described by Lane and a distinctive turban) male peasant dress has dropped many of its features that distinguished broad groups inhabiting the Nile Valley. Now in the place of religious, ethnic, and geographic distinctions, new distinctions of rural and urban, uneducated and educated, naive and sophisticated, are reflected in the styles peasant men wear (see Chapter 6 for details).

---

2. The tarboosh or fez as it is sometimes called is a small truncated cap of red felt. It is of ancient Greek origin. The name "fez" comes from the source of the crimson berry once used to dye the felt. Now only synthetic colors are used. The tarboosh is generally associated in the modern world with Turkish influence during the Ottoman period.

Typical rural folk male's *galabiya*.

Today males of the folk classes wear a simple flowing galabiya with low scooped neckline and an extra V-shaped slit at front center that reveals a finely-striped sidari vest beneath. Another neckline style has this V-shaped opening closed with buttons. The sleeves and skirt both flare funnel-fashion to impressive fullness at wrist and hem line. In the summer, the galabiya is made of colored, striped, or solid cotton material; in the winter, of flannel or wool in darker colors. The heavier galabiya, worn over other layers, is usually decorated at the neckline with rows of braid and perhaps with small rounded braid buttons at front center. The cost of a galabiya made-up varies from a cheap version at about £E 8 or $11 to better ones for £E 20 or 30 to very nice wool galabiyas for perhaps £E 100 or

$140. With minor adaptations noted above, this garment suffices for all folk categories of men of the Nile Valley, affluent (folk level) or poor, Christian or Muslim, landless or landed peasant.

The turban also now is a simple affair ranging from a casually twisted scarf (cotton in summer and wool in winter) on a bare head, to a more carefully wrapped scarf around a foundation cap of crocheted cotton, to the impressively large white turban of the prosperous Nubian. Except in this case, which is associated with a specific group, it is difficult to find clear, large-scale patterns in present-day male headdress: what one observes is that in certain areas head scarves tend to be wound fairly tightly and close to the head, or that a fashion for orange paisley print scarves tends to be found in a particular village and blue in another.[3] These observations however, result mostly from short-lived fashion and even when they seem prevalent, enough contrasting ways of twisting a turban are usually so common as to belie any reasonable level of consistency.

Another common sight is the felt or woolen brown cap of the farmer worn alone without further adornment of head cloths. This leaves the turban's components and make-up largely to the personal idiosyncrasies of the wearer, who decides the appearance he wishes to create whether it be indifference, practicality, affluence, or meticulous attention to the details of grooming and dress. The Arabic expression "to put a turban on someone," which means to make a fool of him, pokes fun at the naive country bumpkin.

When we go beyond the Nile Valley to groups of non-peasant origin, then dress for both males and females features distinctive ways of marking separate identities. Male dress in these communities of special adaptation—bedouin, North Sea Coast, and Red Sea Coast—are discussed in Chapter 5.

3. For example, the head scarf in Sohag and Assyut tends to be wrapped firmly to the sides of the head in a squared-off fashion, rising above the crown of the head in such a way that very little if any of the foundation cap is visible. By contrast in Qena, the head cloth is wrapped with a more visible bulge at the sides of the head, circling the foundation cap much like the rings of a planet. If one spends much time in these areas of Upper Egypt, such markers are almost unconsciously assimilated and used to note the "look" of a person from Sohag or from Qena.

Geographical Understandings in Folk Dress

"Someone else's attire will not look good on you"—Arab proverb

SOME COMMON UNDERSTANDINGS about female folk dress in Egypt, the styles in particular, are recognized[1] as marking geographical place. These styles exist currently or are recent enough to be recognized as a prevalent pattern in a specific region. Sometimes the older forms are worn now only by elderly women or details from the old styles are retained only as elements in newer dresses. In either case, they are part of the cultural repertory which people absorb through socialization and consult when selecting their own dress or interpreting the dress of others.

In the recent past geographic identities have had enough cogency to stimulate distinct regional styles in dress. As regional identities become overwhelmed by other more powerful identities, the regional distinctiveness of dress styles fades and the new identities take on greater power in organizing the dress patterns of people. This is what is happening to some of the geographical markers in parts of Egypt today. Dress provides an accurate measure of where the new identities have taken greatest foothold.

The most common ways that geographical distinctions are marked in Egyptian dress are in large geographical distinctions, by changes in gross silhouette; in regional differences, by general decorative pattern changes in the Delta and by distinctive modesty coverings in Upper Egypt; and in village distinctions, by small differences in the details of dress.

---

1. As with all dress styles, there are limits on the numbers of those who attend completely to the meanings in markers. A remote villager may not realize her dress has significant regional characteristics, for example, because she has never seen any other kind of dress. On the other hand, an established urban elite woman, with a whole array of folk patterns in front of her, may also not recognize regional patterns because folk dress is not something she attends to.

UPPER AND LOWER EGYPTIAN IDENTITIES

The two most common standard models of basic adult female folk dress are the *galabiya bi wist* (dress with a waist) and the *galabiya bi suffra*[2] (a granny style loose-flowing dress with yoked bodice). These styles correspond roughly with the largest geographical distinctions—those of Middle Upper Egypt (*sa'id il wastani*) and the Delta. Deep Upper Egypt (*sa'id il gawwani*) styles are governed by ethnic community distinctions that distribute waisted and yoked styles by other than geographic criteria.[3] (See Chapter 7.)

From Beni Suef to Assyut and sometimes further south the waisted dress (bi wist) is characteristic of this area. It has a joined bodice and full skirt, either gathered or in what is called in Arabic, the *cloche*[4] (bell-shaped) style. The skirt most commonly reaches just below knee length but sometimes dips as low as the floor. The dress waist tends to be higher than the natural waistline in order to accommodate heavy and pregnant women. The sleeves may be gathered or narrow, following the contours of the arms closely. They are always long, three-quarter length or more.

Variety of decoration occurs on the bodice and neckline of the waisted dress. These are often outlined in braid, shirred with rows of gathers, or piped to appear like a collar. Some of the favorite necklines are called *murabba* (square), *sabaa* (seven), *maftuh* (open), and frangi (foreign). Each name describes the effect it creates (seven in Arabic forms a "V"), except frangi which simply indicates that the neckline is topped with a collar. Sometimes two patterns are combined as when the lower edge of "square" is extended with a "seven" to a shallow "V." A variety of these details may be found in the same village, though from time to time one may become more stylish than another, or a particular seamstress may be more adept at one than another. (See Chapter 6 on Youth and Maturity.)

The yoked granny dress is the style that extends through the heartland of the Delta down to and including the total urban area of Cairo. The style has full sleeves and a flow of material that falls in gathers to the ankles from a round or square yoke. The yoke differs in the shallowness or depth of its plunge, in its neckline's decoration, type of closure, and in the presence or absence of a collar.

It is interesting to note that in the long history of Western fashions, it is

2. The most common bi suffra or granny dress is an unelaborated modern style that will be discussed in Chapter 6. Older Delta styles employ tucks and various bodice treatments that are slightly different from the fully yoked style but in all cases they make no attempt to develop a truly waisted look. So in this sense bi suffra is a convenient and accurate contrast to bi wist.

3. Some people told me that in Assyut waisted styles were first used by Christians and for a time distinguished Christians from Muslims. Present-day usage, however, does not make that distinction in the villages around Assyut (see Chapter 7).

4. Note the adoption of the French word. French terms are frequently used to designate details of folk dress. See later in the chapter for more about these usages.

Street scene in the lower-
class quarters of Cairo:
woman in foreground
wearing Upper Egyptian
waisted dress, and
woman in background
left with Lower Egyptian
granny dress.

rare to see unwaisted styles. The allure of dress for women is to display the figure
attractively which requires fitted rather than loose unstructured styles. In the last
two hundred years, the major unwaisted styles have been the empire dress which
was the fashion during the period of the first Empire (1804–1814) in the Napoleonic era, and the boyish look of the flapper era in the first decades of the twentieth century. The Delta granny dress, therefore, seems more appropriate in the
context of Islamic codes of dress that are interpreted to require obscuring of the
female figure. It is not simple coincidence that Egyptians found the empire dress
so appealing when Napoleon's following trooped through Egypt.

The silhouettes of waisted and granny styles in Upper Egypt and Lower Egypt
make them immediately and visibly distinguishable as coming from different
regions. Head coverings of specific types help to confirm the identification, but
at present there is so much variety in the way people cover their heads that this

Waisted dress (*Galabiya bi wist*), right figure. Yoked granny dress (*Galabiya bi suffra*), left figure.

item of dress can no longer be depended upon for positive identification of geographic origins. However, there are some general characteristics of head coverings that relate a tendency to geographic place.

All peasant women wear some form of head covering from the time they are young children. There are three most common kinds of basic head covering (not including at this point what are termed here as modesty garments). Head coverings can be worn alone or in combinations. The most basic covering is a head scarf (*sharb*),[5] a square of brightly colored, plain, or black material, some-

5. Originally the sharb was tied around the crown of the head with two of its four end pieces crossed and brought to the front and knotted low on the forehead. Now interestingly, this way of tying the scarf is found more often among the bedouin, among rather remote villagers, and one version of the style is found in a headdress of fundamentalist style (see Chapter 7). The *mandiil*

Galabiya bi wist with *shaal:* Middle Upper Egypt.

times but not always worked along the edges with crochet, beading, or tassels. The square is folded in a triangle, placed over the head, covering the hair at the forehead, crossed under the hair at the back of the neck, and finally tied in a small knot over the forehead. The knot may gather several tassels attractively over the face or when covered by another garment leave a lump that provides a fetching fullness to an otherwise skinned look. Many Delta women wear only this head covering much of the time, which with the voluminous gathers of their granny dresses, and the shoulder-exaggerating shape of the dresses' yokes, gives the appearance of massive bulk topped by a tightly swathed, delicately balancing little oval.

Another large number of Delta women add to the scarf the second com-

was another form of head scarf, three-cornered, that was used to cover the head at night, and was usually tied under the chin.

Galabiya bi suffra with *tarha:* Delta.

mon head covering, the tarha, a long and flowing narrow rectangle of light-weight cloth two to four meters long. The tarha, usually black, is wrapped around the head several times from chin to crown, and the remaining meter or more hangs down the center of the back. Though the tarha even more adequately covers the head than the scarf, including also the neck area of the wearer, it has more than just practical uses. It comes closest to being the floating veil of a houri, trailing gracefully in the wake of its wearer, constantly being rearranged or flipped over the shoulder in the pretty gestures that young girls in particular like to employ. It floats with the wearer and can be drawn shyly over the mouth when meeting a stranger. It enhances the Delta granny dress by restoring to the wearer a more appropriately proportioned head, if she twists its folds in a flattering way.

Middle Upper Egyptian women also often wear a scarf or a tarha, especially

Head scarf (*mandiil* or *sharb*), right figure. Head veil (*tarha*), left figure.

during their daily activities working around the house or hauling water. But their "finished" look on more formal occasions (or even on everyday occasions) tends to include the *shaal* (shawl), a ready-made fringed cotton, rayon, or velvet two-meter square of material, sometimes colored but usually black. Because it is of heavy-weight material the shawl is not tied but rather folded in a triangle and placed either across the shoulders or more often across the head and flowing down to the shoulders. The nun-like effect is accentuated further by the practice of wrapping the head and neck area underneath the shawl with a length of black lighter-weight material. The over-all silhouette of this Upper Egyptian ensemble thus becomes a set of blending curves from the tip of the head to the shoulder, in at the waist and out again to the hem of the skirt, with the only abrupt transition at the point where the legs protrude from under the dress.

Tarha and scarf on a young woman in the Delta.

The body outlines are largely preserved, if sometimes only in a modified way.

Shawls are not a monopoly of Upper Egypt though they are most commonly found in those areas of the South. Delta women also sometimes wear them especially in the colder months of the year, and even sometimes enjoy twisting lighter-weight fringed shawls into turbans on their heads.

The typical Delta dress, therefore, has a silhouette that is commodious and conceals the human form underneath; the Middle Upper Egypt dress preserves the form through the folds of the cloth by hugging the chest, arms, and waist.

REGIONAL IDENTITIES

The next overlay of more specific geographical identities is located by regional reference points. Again there is a notable difference between much of the Delta and Upper Egypt.

Shawl (*shaal*).

The cultivated areas of Egypt which are also the main centers of population have been likened to a lotus blossom spreading out along the several tributaries of the Nile to form the broad agricultural flat lands of the Delta. This Delta blossom extends from a long slender Upper Egyptian stalk, the main branch of the Nile that curves through the rest of Southern Egypt into the Sudan. Near Cairo is the junction where the main branch divides and spreads out into the blossom of the Delta.

Delta inhabitants are connected by short distances with other villages, larger towns, even big cities. Their orientation is therefore often multi-directional but always has at least one urban focus. Upper Egyptians live primarily along a north-south axis formed by the Nile, and they usually look in one of those two directions to the nearest town where goods are sold, bought, and sometimes bartered.

Dress reflects these different orientations. In the Delta, the most socially significant large-scale geographical boundaries roughly overlap with the political boundaries of some of the governorates. There is evidence in the way people talk about its inhabitants that reveal their sense of the uniqueness of each governorate. For example, the eastern governorate of Sharqiya is remembered for the historic day the people "invited the train to lunch," a reference to the inauguration of a new train line, but at the same time a sly comment on both the generosity and the reputed stupidity of the people of Sharqiya. Similar comments are made about the uniqueness of the people of Menufiya and Boheira.

Until recently, decorative details of the unwaisted Delta dress style were critical in identifying areas in most of the major governorates of the Delta. Older women still sometimes wear these styles and one finds traces of their designs in contemporary dress. There are several main patterns.[6]

Boheira

The style found in Boheira is characterized by the outline of the bust in wide piping of a color that usually contrasts with the color of the dress. The square neckline is outlined in several lines of piping that extend down to enhance the curves of the breast. Three tucks extend down the center of the dress to prevent too unwieldy a fullness, but they are compensated in part by small gathers at either side under the bodice. The sleeves are wide, maintaining their fullness with one or more horizontal tucks at the shoulder and three vertical tucks extending to a cuff-like decorative ribbon with piped edging at the wrist. A short ruffle of about eight inches trails slightly longer behind the wearer.

There is considerable variety in the decorative elements found in the bodice of the Boheira dress. A number of common ones are *darabiya* (line of pleats), *mraayaat* (mirrors), *fawaniis* (lanterns), *kubbayyaat* (glasses) and *fanagiin* (cups). The dress is always found in colors, either solids or patterned. This style of high-waisted dress, called embire in Arabic most certainly takes its inspiration from the French invasion of Egypt in the late 18th century.[7] The decorative piping even retains the deep decolletage of the French style, but modestly fills in with contrasting material the areas where bare flesh appeared in the French version. Plumpness is particularly admired in Boheira and the fitted upper sections of the dress help to reveal the plumpness that other styles of granny dress conceal.

6. I am indebted to Shahira Mehrez who first drew my attention to these Delta dresses and gave me much interesting information on their details.
7. In these areas, as Shahira Mehrez points out, the people rather than using Arabic terms use the French words *soutage* for braid and *orangi* for the color orange. Mary Megalli, a boat enthusiast, points out that Egypt is a graveyard for old boat terminology. The same seems also to be true for dress terminology.

Boheira Dress.

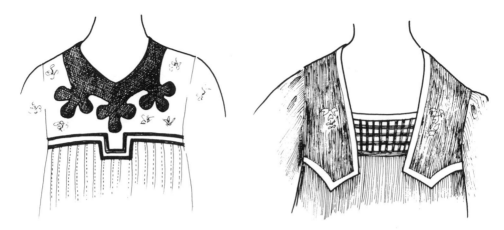

Bodice treatment in Delta dresses: Sharqiya, right figure; Gharbiya, left figure.

The bedouin tribal origins of many of the people of Boheira perhaps explains their love of brightly colored prints and their infrequent use of somber ones.

In parts of Boheira province farther from urban centers such as areas west of Damenhour, this dress is still commonly found today. The most common contemporary pattern has two rows of decorative piping forming a "W" at the neckline reminiscent of the decolletage mentioned above, and three rows of horizontal piping immediately below the "W" that forms a tight band across the bust. (See Chapter 6 on youthful *moda* styles and Chapter 5 for coastal influences on Boheira styles.)

Gharbiya

The Gharbiya dress has a square yoke marked at the lower edge by two rows of braid with a center crenellation. The neckline is trimmed with velvet inset to form three downward spikes ending commonly in velvet trefoils, the whole outline marked with a braid edging. Though the dress is loose-fitting in the general granny style, a number of narrow vertical tucks extend from bodice to below waist level to preserve a trace of the feminine shape beneath. A large ruffle edges the bottom of the dress from mid-calf to floor and is decorated with braid at the seam connecting the ruffle with the main body of the dress.

Tucks on the sleeve at the shoulder make a slight cap effect that accentuates the broadness of the woman. Three tucks along the length of the sleeve only reduce the sleeve's fullness minimally. The sleeve ends in a velvet cuff that is again outlined in braid. Three one-inch tucks above the ruffle uniformly circle

Detail of dress from Gharbiya.

the skirt. Often the dress has side openings near the sleeves for ease in breast feeding. This dress is often seen in dark colors but patterned or lighter solid color materials are also sometimes found.

Traces of this style are still found in the occasional square-yoked dress found in Gharbiya and in another governorate of the Delta, Kafr il Sheikh. Gharbiya and Kafr il Sheikh were joined into one governorate during the period before the Revolution, named Fawadiya. It was not until about 1948 that Kafr il Sheikh was carved out as a separate governorate. Dress of the region has not caught up with the political boundaries or, perhaps more accurately, it has not been necessary to reflect a unique identity for the governorate. The dress of the fledgling governorate takes its inspiration from a number of sources (see Chapter 8) that have since taken on more important significance than regional values.

Menufiya

The standard Menufiya dress has a square yoke, rather than the common modern curved yoke; it is a full granny dress with short ruffle and even hem. The dress is often made up in a solid color with contrasting piping, frequently of the same color but a darker shade. Tucks at the wrist draw in the fullness of the sleeve, and tucks above the ruffle allow for lengthening the dress if it becomes too short.

Detail of dress from Sharqiya.

Sharqiya

Sharqiya has also a variety of decorative styles. Most characteristic, however, is the bodice decoration called *shebabiik*[8] (literally windows) that insinuates itself into Sharqiya dresses in a variety of ways. It is a lattice-work pattern forming small openings that reveal the flesh beneath. It may be found bordering the slightly pointed but otherwise square neckline, or it may extend in two double lines vertically along the breasts, or it may appear as a lattice-work square just below the neckline. Almost always this "window" work is accompanied with other decorative detail, either in piping outline or with gold-beaded flowers sewn in a square around the neck.

The Sharqiya dress is one of the most elegant designs. Small vertical tucks at the shoulder provide fullness without the broadness of other designs. A sweeping train is created by a generous ruffle that drops down as tucks in the front of the dress disappear in the back. Some claim the train allows women to bend over more modestly; others note that in conservative communities it is thought modest for a woman to erase her footsteps as she walks so she leaves nothing behind for a stranger male to see. The Sharqiya dress is usually found in black only.

8. Shahira Mehrez points out that the "windows" are reminiscent of the "entre-deux" pattern found on the bodice of costumes worn by nineteenth-century Europeans.

Sharqiya dress.

Bodice variation: Sharqiya.

Kalubiya

Kalubiya, just north of Cairo, surrounded by four governorates and the city of Cairo, hardly has a distinctive flavor of its own any more. Still villagers claim a Kalubiya style modelled on many of the same features as its surrounding neighbors. A piped, accentuated high waist and gathered front (but no tucks) is similar to the embire of Boheira. The deep decolletage differs however. Triangular cut-outs bordering the neckline and outlined also with piping remind one of the square shababiik patterns of Sharqiya. High stand-up leg-of-mutton sleeves are similar to those found in Alexandria (see Chapter 5). A modest ruffle with the obligatory tucks above where it joins the dress completes the outfit.

From the descriptions above and the accompanying illustrations it becomes apparent that the Delta draws its regional distinctions most visibly through differences in the decorative designs of the bodice.

Upper Egyptians with their orientation toward the north-south axis of the river and less to larger-bounded regional entities identify their differences in an-

Kalubiya dress.

other way. They maintain broad areas of basically similar dress but rely on the inspiration of regional market towns for distinctive modesty garments. It is in these towns that many such garments can be bought ready-made, or if not ready-made, at least the raw materials for their construction can be found.

Distances in the Delta are short and the multitude of influences from urban, coastal, and desert areas great. Wearing the characteristic style of one's area means rejecting the other possibilities open. In Upper Egypt domains of influence tend to be more discrete, separated as they are by greater distances and fewer sources of competition. From the focal town a style radiates out as far as the people are interested in accepting its influence or until it meets the competing force of another town's radiation. Then the mutually supporting conditions of consumer demand and availability of the style serve to continue a pattern almost indefinitely.

This Upper Egyptian pattern is most clearly seen in styles of modesty garments but it can also be seen in other aspects of dress. For example, if one compares dresses of the Fayoum oasis with dresses of Beni Suef (its nearest market connection along the Nile), and dresses of Bayad (across the Nile and north but with a nearby ferry service to Beni Suef), one finds an almost identically detailed bodice decoration in identically waisted dresses. It appears that this style has spread from the Beni Suef centrum with no thought to distinguishing the oasis of Fayoum from the Nile Valley, or the east from the west bank of the Nile. Later we will see how the majority of other oases have continued to maintain characteristic styles that until recently served to distinguish them from the Valley. What is interesting in the Fayoum example is that the influences on dress have followed an older connection between Fayoum and Beni Suef along a major canal, rather than the modern road link to Cairo (see Chapter 5 for a similar example in the Delta). The totally different granny dress, more typical of Cairo, has not taken hold in the Fayoum in any significant way. Such evidence demonstrates, perhaps as well as any other, the magnetism of market towns for isolated Upper Egyptian villagers.

Regional distinctions in Upper Egypt are more frequently marked by modesty garments that roughly distinguish hinterlands dominated by important towns. The term "modesty garment" is in some ways a misnomer. It is a garment that is not, strictly speaking, part of a woman's minimal outfit though at times she would feel very uncomfortable going without it. The garment is worn under certain conditions and certain circumstances which will be clarified in Chapter 6. Similarly it is not always possible to make a clear distinction between a modesty garment and other pieces of apparel since many elements in dress and head coverings have their modesty component as well. To simplify the terminology used here, when an item of clothing might not always be worn around the house but would be put on to appear before strangers, to make a formal visit to the market

Returning from the well: detail of dress in Bayad.

or to friends, it is designated a modesty garment. Many current modesty styles became fashionable during Ottoman rule in Egypt.

Basically there are three styles of modesty garment: shawls, cloaks, and over-dresses. They almost invariably are black or of somber hue. In most of the Delta, women wear a black yoked over-dress similar to the basic dress of the Delta when they feel the need, which is not always, to wear a modesty garment. It is Upper Egyptians who are more likely to wear shawls and cloaks over a black dress typical of their region. The local terms used to describe modesty garments tend to be vague, in the same way that the term "covering" would be non-specific in English. Below are examples of the most common varieties of Upper Egyptian modesty garments along with the city names with which they are commonly associated. Their incidence is not so invariable[9] that one expects them only to be found at these locations. People are likely to say, "Oh yes, that's the style they wear in X town."

9. Cities and towns serve as focal points for an original style but in themselves they are the least consistent in dress style, reflecting the wide range of their inhabitants' socio-economic levels and sophistication.

Assyut and Minya

The shawl (shaal) as a modesty garment is exactly the same as the shaal described above as head covering, except that it is normally black[10] as a modesty garment. Shawls as modesty garments may top scarf and tarha head coverings, or as head coverings they may be topped by other modesty garments. The shaal, ready-made, cost £E 1.50 to £E 2.00 in 1978 but like other items of dress has increased significantly since then.

Assyut

In villages near Assyut and particularly to the south is found the *shugga,* a distinctive wide flowing, floor-length cloak, a style that is said to have originated during the period of Mamluk rule in Egypt. The shugga's capacity to conceal is so complete that it is impossible to know what is worn underneath. It envelops the wearer's head, shoulders, and body in a shimmer of light-weight silk or synthetic material of similar weight that gives the impression of a floating balloon in full motion.

The shugga is made by joining two lengths of cloth along parallel selvages, then folding the two ends to center front, seaming at the shoulders so a front opening is created. The cloak is very similar to that described by Lane (1954, orig. 1908) as the hubbara. The shugga is found interspersed with the shawl both within towns and between towns. Its incidence appears to mark affluence because of the expense involved in purchasing the six or seven meters of silk or other fine material used in its construction. Occasionally even in towns some distance south of Assyut one finds the shugga in well-to-do village families. In other countries of the Middle East, the shugga (or hubbara as it is called there) is found as a remnant of Turkish occupation. The hands are generally occupied in holding the slippery material in front of the face so that little of the woman's features are visible.

In the Assyut Governorate's remote southwestern rural town of Ghaneyem a complicated version of the shugga is still commonly worn by some middle-aged and older women. This shugga consists of a floor-length gathered skirt with long panel extending from the skirt's waist that drapes in two bunches over the hips (French "shepherdess" style), is thrown up over the head and then falls around the figure in a way identical to the contemporary shugga. (This style is similar to the two-piece hubbara with skirt and hip length shawl-covering worn several decades ago in Assyut.) Some of the women in this conservative town also wear

10. Young girls often wear bright-colored shawls, orange, or green and red striped, as ordinary head coverings.

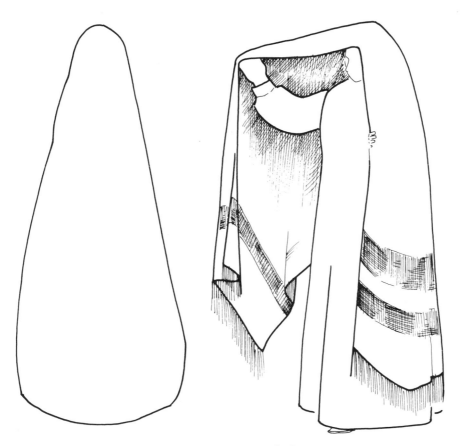

Hubbara, right figure. *Shugga* (back view), left figure.

light-weight black veils to cover their entire faces. Their tarhas are often decorated elaborately at the edges with beaded laced macrame.

Sohag

In villages near Sohag one finds the *birda,* a rectangle of approximately 1½ × 4 meters. It comes in a variety of materials from the coarsely woven wool versions of farm women to more elegant and fine versions made of "smoking," rayon, or fine wool woven by more sophisticated village or town women. The heavy wool birda may be dark brown with a stripe of a different contrasting color such as red or green, placed just a few inches from a generous fringe at either end. Some versions have a continuous alteration of stripes in brown and black. Birdas of finer textiles frequently are seen with the white-printed selvage declaring its

Woman with beaded *tarha*
near Qena.

foreign source of manufacture. From a distance this printing appears to be simply
an edge stripe. The owner wears it over the crown of her head and falling over
the shoulders or she may attach one end at the waist and throw the other over
her head. Even though people generally associate the birda with the area near
Sohag, perhaps because it is first seen there as one moves south, its incidence
occurs in regions as far south as Idfu and Kom Ombo. The name birda refers
to the material of striped woven wool called *bird*. It was said to have been worn
by the Prophet. The word *bird* is said by local people to take its meaning from
the root connoting "cold" because of its characteristically heavy weight.

Qena

   A distinctive modesty garment seen commonly in Qena and extensively
in the stretch 20 kilometers south of Qena on the West bank of the Nile is the
nishra. It is a large finely woven wool rectangle of black background with fine

Detail of *hubbara* worn
over a *jubba*.

plaid of red and white lines that costs more than £E 10. The narrow edges of the
nishra are fringed.

It is not accidental that Qena, which served as the traditional Nile caravan
crossroads between the Red Sea Coast and Libya, should be one of the sources
of goods for the oasis to the west. The same nishra, often simply called futa (cloth)
in the oasis, makes up part of the traditional costume of Bahriya oasis, but combined with oasis style rather than Nile valley dresses. Its incidence on the oasis
side of the Nile up to a point just about opposite the important caravan juncture
of Qus[11] is suggestive of the significance of supply routes in the distribution of

11. Travellers from the oases to the Red Sea Coast usually took one of the caravan routes to the
Nile Valley, arriving at Cairo, Samalut near Minya, or Farshut near Nag Hamadi and proceeding

Jubba or *tobe*.

a garment (in Upper Egypt by caravan, and in Lower Egypt by water routes).

Between Qena and Luxor also is seen occasionally another less common modesty covering, resembling a large yellow, white, and black plaid rectangular cloth, similar to a tablecloth, that completely envelops the body. This *ferka,* as it is called, is used also in the Sudan and sometimes comes in other colors.

Women in Qena who do not wear the nishra wear the birda over their waisted dresses. One almost never sees the coarsely woven wool birdas of Sohag with their

by boat to Qift or Qus where they could pick up the caravan crossing the Eastern Desert to Qusayr on the Red Sea.

characteristic stripes, however. The birda of Qena is almost always black and usually of a finer grain wool. Underneath the women often wear tarhas with tassels or beaded macrame edgings, topping a small scarf tied in a knot at the crown. One variation is a black tarha with red striped edging similar to a heavier version seen in the oases of the Kharga to Bahriya complex, and also commonly in faraway Yemen across the Red Sea.

Luxor

In the conservative region north and south of Luxor one finds much more frequent use of special modesty garments, worn even while engaged in such everyday tasks as bringing water from the Nile. They may cover waisted dresses that are ankle length, with trailing ruffles. In and near Luxor one sees the large and enveloping rectangular (1½ meter by 3 or 4 meters) hubbara competing with the still generally common modesty style of Middle Upper Egypt, the waisted black dress and shawl.

The hubbara[12] can be one of the most beautiful of the modesty garments when it is woven in a medium-weight black silk, or light-weight rayon synthetic with ribbed stripe and twisted fringe on the two narrower edges. Some of these fine hubbaras are all black but some have stripes of deep purple that add to the shimmery appearance of the cloth. Other less elegant hubbaras are made of coarse material which makes them almost indistinguishable from light wool birdas. The hubbara is manufactured in Akhmiin and Nagada. Women explain that it is normally worn with one edge folded back in double thickness over the head and a single thickness over shoulders and back.[13]

In conservative villages south and north of Luxor, the large formless hubbara is often worn over the practical caftanlike jubba.[14] As a garment the jubba is complicated and difficult to understand at first glance. With close inspection, how-

12. Assyutis tell me that the hubbara at one time was a two-piece modesty outfit worn by town people. There was a black A-line over-skirt, with accompanying top draped over and tied behind the head and falling over the shoulders to the waist in a cloak-like effect. This two-piece style is reminiscent of a walking suit that was popular in Europe at the end of the nineteenth century. Assyutis in the early decades of the twentieth century prided themselves on dressing in the European fashion. One source for their inspiration was the missionary school marms who taught in the Protestant Mission schools there. The two-piece hubbara, called a *sharshaf,* is still a common style worn in the Yemeni capital of Sanaa.
13. While the hubbara is often worn over the jubba, women say the urban style *melaya* (see Chapter 6) is never worn over a jubba, only over a basic folk dress or a foreign dress. Such conventions are often based on combinations that people categorize as modern or traditional.
14. Jubba is also the name given to an over-robe tying at the waist that was worn by men but which is rarely seen now except on hotel bellhops or restaurant waiters.

ever, the ingenuity of its design becomes apparent. It is, in effect, a birda constructed in a way that forms a loose dress through artful sewing of seams. The birda is folded in half to form the right side seam. Along the top edge a section is left unseamed for the wearer's right arm but sewn on either side of the neck to form an opening. The edge at left shoulder is unseamed, falling away at the shoulder in a graceful drape of fringed edge. Near the ankle a small seam or sewn-on strap holds the two edges of the jubba together. The neck edge is often surrounded by braid decoration. A deep oval neckline and further center slit to below the breast gives freedom of movement to the garment, as does the fact that the square is so large that it droops over the shoulders causing the corners of the top edge to fall almost to the wrist in a normal standing position.

Women drawing water from the Nile take up the bottom edges and twist them expertly around their waists. Returning with the water balanced on their heads, the slits along the top edge allow the material to gather and drape at the shoulders, like a sleeveless tunic, freeing both arms to steady the water. Used in this way the bag-like jubba is normally made of medium-weight sateen or heavy polished cotton that shimmers slightly as the wearer moves, or it may be made from any of the usual birda materials. It is always black. In these villages near Luxor, then, one may see the women wearing their everyday waisted dresses (called tawb there) with shaal, or with layered jubba and hubbara.

Isna

Near Isna, a distinct modesty garment called tawb (to be distinguished from the tawb waisted dress near Luxor) is found that approximates the *bedla* style of Sharqiya Governorate (see Chapter 6) and may or may not be related. The Isna dress is an A-line ankle-length dress with sleeves that are wide at the wrists, similar to the rural male's galabiya. The neck oval is extended with an opening in center front for ease in slipping over the head. The dress is made from a heavy cotton or sateen. The terms tawb (often spelled *tobe*) and jubba are both general terms for outer garments found throughout the Middle East. In Upper Egypt however, the people use them for specific styles.

It is likely that there is a connection between the Isna dress and oasis dress (see Chapter 4) since Isna was one of the main connecting points with the Nile Valley for caravans coming from the oases of the Western Desert. Combine the basic shape of the Isna tawb with embroidery and the resulting dress is very like the example of the Nubian *thawb* (another spelling variant) found in the Folkloric Museum of Cairo (see Chapter 4). Both dresses could be incipient forms of the oasis dress.[15]

15. There are other possible hypotheses, of course. The oasis dress could have inspired the Valley

Roughly speaking the garments above reflect middle-level geographical identities. The people of a region understand and attend to these differences, but
it is not likely that many people of the Delta know much about the distinctions
of Upper Egypt and vice versa, nor is it likely that middle-class and upper-class
inhabitants of towns are conscious of the full significance of peasant dress in their
areas. The messages are therefore tuned to special in-groups, the folk classes of
Upper or Lower Egypt themselves. People of these classes often recognize that
distinctions are being made, without consciously courting the distinctions themselves. For individuals, dress may be thought of more as a way of identifying one-
self with a valued group than as a sign of rejecting another group. The latter
may occur as an unintended by-product of the first.

One time, while visiting a village in Upper Egypt, I noticed that one among
a group of young women I was talking to was wearing a clearly identifiable Delta
dress from Sharqiya. She was not surprised that a well-travelled outsider should
ask about her dress and recognize her origins. She explained that she was recently
married to a cousin who had come searching for a bride among his Delta relatives
and this dress was part of her wedding trousseau. Up until the time I spoke to
her, she still felt the style and the cut of Delta patterns were far superior to garments
in the south, and was not interested in changing to a different style.

Another time in a lower-class neighborhood in Cairo, I recognized a dress
from deep within the Delta, and again asked the woman if she wasn't from that
area. To my disappointment she answered that she was born and rasied in Cairo.
I was convinced of the origin of the style and so asked further about where she
had obtained the dress. Again came the disappointing answer that she had made
the dress herself. I was about to give up on the puzzle when she mentioned that
she had learned to sew from her mother who had indeed grown up in the area
I had mentioned.

Regional styles which are identifiable most certainly have some connection
with their place of origin no matter how out of context one may find them. For
example, on the road between Assyut and Ghaneyem one comes, at the curve
of the road, to a village called Zawya. There the women wear a colorful Boheira
square-yoked dress with three-pronged neck piping that floats down to a wide
ruffle at hemline. It is unlike all others of the generally "waisted" region. Almost
certainly in their past people migrated from the Delta to this region of Upper
Egypt where the land is now being, and in the past has been, extensively reclaimed. There in Zawya the women cling to their old dress style with more
tenacity than their sisters of origin who have now been influenced by sophisticate
styles from neighboring towns. For the women of Zawya the dress has come to
symbolize their separateness from other groups in the vicinity.

---

dress. The Isna dress could, for example, be a more sober version of the decorative oasis dress, befit-
ting the more somber tastes of the valley peasant.

LOCAL IDENTITIES

At the microcosmic level of villages, distinctions become even more subtle. Some villagers appear to make no distinctions between themselves and other villages at all. In some villages the distinctions are probably more circumstantial than real, a product of the different sewing skills of village seamstresses or different traditions that have developed in those particular villages (see Chapter 5 for generational changes in a village). In some cases villagers point out that people in their own village dress more modestly than another village. The next village may counter by claiming itself to be more modern.

It is probably true to say that when subtle differences do exist, for whatever reason, they are seized upon as ways of identifying the origins of unknown people seen perhaps at a regional market, or walking along a road. One village in particular took pains to explain to me how their dresses differed from a nearby village and were quite offended to think I might consider them equally beautiful. I offer this example as an illustration of how subtle village-level differences can be. The main point is that inhabitants attend to the differences, conform to the distinctive elements in their own village's dress, and invest them with an aura of moral or aesthetic superiority. Again the point is equally well made that villagers are first and foremost conforming to their own group's norms and only secondarily rejecting the norms of another group.

Abu Ruwwash and Bortus

These two villages lie in a pocket of communities to the west of the Nile near the Giza pyramids and bounded in the north by the bend in the river where the Boheira branch suddenly snakes out to the left. These villages on the very periphery of sand and cultivated area have historically supplemented their farming activities with the products of their looms. Modern industries include those of Harraniya and Kirdasa, which are world famous, but surrounding villages too still hang out hanks of brightly dyed wool and women everywhere are seen carrying their hand spindles, while men and children operate the creaking hand looms. This region is especially picturesque in terms of peasant dress which is some of the most attractive and vividly colored of the country.

The villages of Abu Ruwwash and Bortus are about eight miles apart as the crow flies, somewhat longer on the tortuous roads of the area. At first glance the dresses of Bortus and Abu Ruwwash look the same. Both basically follow the granny style, long and full, with wide gathered sleeves and square-yoked bodice. A large ruffle at the hem droops to trail longer in the back. According to the inhabitants of Bortus however, the similarities end there. In Bortus, for example there are three small horizontal tucks in the front of the dress just above the

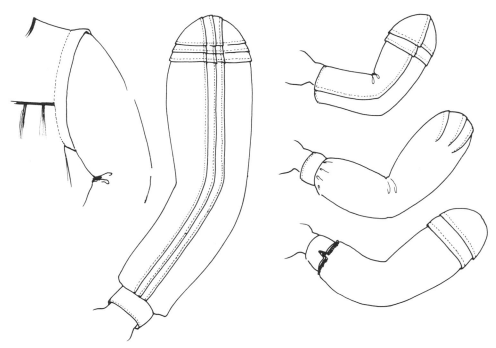

Sleeve treatments in the Delta: Bortus, center figure; Abu Ruwwash, left figure.

ruffle and no tucks behind so that a longer dip in the train results. In the village of Abu Ruwwash the three tucks in the front become two in the back making a less exaggerated train. Zig-zag braid covers the seam of the ruffle in Abu Ruwwash but not in Bortus. The opening for nursing comes at the center front in Abu Ruwwash and in two slits on the sides in Bortus, "spoiling" the continuity of the yoke where much of the decorative work is concentrated.

Bortus people claim that their yokes are covered with more embroidery in flowers of colored thread, or black or gold beads, or sequins. The people of Abu Ruwwash use the same materials but embroider circles and lines more than flowers. In both villages women sew the dresses and men specialists do the machine embroidery of threads. What may be most significant in terms of recognition of the two styles of dress is the sleeve treatment at the shoulder. In Abu Ruwwash a large tuck gives a modified pinafore effect at the shoulder while in Bortus small tucks spread the fullness of the sleeve but do not conceal the join between sleeve and shoulder.

What is common to many women in both villages yet not so common to those wearing Nile valley costumes generally is the method of tying head coverings with the knot outside and low at the back of the head, giving a rounded cap-like effect with the streamers of the material hanging down the back of the wearer. This way of wearing a head covering is more often seen among bedouin.

Local distinctions like those in Bortus and Abu Ruwwash, it would seem, are not systematically created, and when they exist for circumstantial or other reasons they may not be exploited by people as distinctive markers unless there are other reasons for doing so. In the more densely populated areas where Abu Ruwwash and Bortus are located, one senses a competitiveness between towns, even flaring sometimes into local rivalries over their common textile interests. There are few natural boundaries to separate and give definition to these communities. It is probably reasonable to argue that under such circumstances distinguishing details take on a cogency they might not otherwise possess.

The Nile Valley and Oases

"Birds of a feather flock together"—Arab proverb

RECOGNIZING GEOGRAPHIC MARKERS in dress is usually a skill absorbed by people simply as a matter of growing up and wearing what everyone else in a region wears. The use of an outfit as a marker is tested in such cases only when it comes in contact with other regional costumes at a market town or if for some reason its territory is invaded by another costume design. Another set of costumes, those reflecting community attachments, is somewhat different. For these distinctive patterns to persist depends on one or more adversary designs to which a contrast can be drawn. The allegiance to community which spawns their invention in the first place also prevents easy acceptance of outsider patterns except under unusual circumstances.

Peasant life in the Central Nile Valley and the Delta is the heart of the Egyptian economy even though urban populations (44 percent of the total) are growing at such a rate as will soon overtake the ratios of rural inhabitants. The uniquely Egyptian style has been shaped and tested over thousands of years of the agricultural experience. Even so, the picture of Egypt is not complete without acknowledging the encroachment of marginally agricultural peoples along the edges of the most fertile agricultural center line. These people include the bedouins of the Eastern and Western deserts, the Sinai and the North Coast; the Nubians of the South; coastal dwellers; and the inhabitants of the ring of oases to the west of the Nile Valley and in Siwa near the Libyan border. Each of these communities retains distinctive elements in their dress that visibly distinguish them from other Egyptians. The following two chapters will describe some of their differences.

By starting first with the Nubians, we can continue the train of the previous chapter by moving south up the Nile. The contemporary Nubian story begins several decades ago when the bulk of their tribes were spread out along the Nile from Aswan south to the Sudan. Even though Nubians had previously engaged primarily in farming, the three raisings of the Aswan Dam in 1912, 1933, and 1970 completely eliminated the agricultural lands of Lower Nubia and forced the evacuation of Egyptian Nubians to less fertile areas in Kom Ombo, in the present-day Governorate of Aswan. As early as the 1933 raising of the dam, agriculture had been reduced in Nubia to a marginal four-month crop because of detrimental irrigation policies. With each displacement of Nubian populations, more and more of the able-bodied men left their families behind and sought service and clerical positions in urban centers of Egypt. By the time new irrigation schemes had been created, Nubians were well established in their urban jobs, leaving their fields uncultivated or leased to Sa'idi[1] sharecroppers (Kennedy 1977: 27–28).

Traditionally, the home of the "real"[2] Sa'idis (Upper Egyptians of mixed Arab and African origins) was located in the areas from south of Assyut to Aswan, while the Nubians occupied the areas south of Aswan. While the fair-skinned, rounder-faced Christians of Middle Upper Egypt are also sometimes referred to as Sa'idis by Northerners, the distinctions of who are "true" Sa'idis become more subtle and important as one moves south. From Sohag, Qena, and Luxor on southward people retain sharp Arab or bedouin features and their skins become increasingly darker. By Esna, Edfu, Daraw, and Kom Ombo this tendency reaches its apex in the Ga'afra Sa'idis who are thought by themselves and Nubians to be related to the Nubians. They provide the transitional link between the Arabs to the North and the Nubians to the south in such a way that makes it difficult to draw a clear line on the basis of physical appearance alone.

We know only that before 1963, with the exception of a few resettled villages, few Nubians lived north of Aswan (Fernea and Gerster:1973). After 1963 and the resettlement in Kom Ombo large numbers of Nubians occupied areas formerly inhabited mainly by Sa'idis. Nubian willingness to lease land to the Sa'idis intensified their relationship with each other in a way that demonstrated the different subsistence adjustments the two populations were making.

South of Kom Ombo begins the area of fairly consistent contemporary use of Nubian dress patterns. Around Kom Ombo itself there are three distinct dress styles: two that Nubians wear and one that characterizes the Sa'idi peasants. Though Sa'idis appear much earlier as one moves south toward Kom Ombo, the heavy concentrations of the Sa'idi dress become most apparent when they come in contact with significant numbers of Nubians near Kom Ombo.

---

1. Generally speaking, Sa'idi (Upper Egyptian) is the contrast of Bahrawi (a person from the Delta). Sa'idi here is used as a contrast to Nubian. Sa'idis are a narrower category of Muslim Upper Egyptian peasants.
2. The "real" Sa'idis come from *Sa'id al-gawwani,* Deep Upper Egypt, as opposed to *Sa'id al-wastani,* Middle Upper Egypt.

SA'IDIS

South of Luxor, yoked granny dresses similar to those of the Delta begin to appear regularly as the distinguishing feature of the peasant Sa'idi. The dress in this setting is called a *tawb* (the term often used in Upper Egypt for galabiya) *sharqawi* (coming from Sharqiya governorate). The name reflects the close connections the Sa'idis have maintained historically with the Delta Sharqawis. The connection moves in two directions: the Sa'idis migrating to more fertile areas of Sharqiya to farm and Shargawi women being brought back as wives to the Sa'id. Both areas have felt the impact of the dress of the other — Sharqiya in its tendency to a greater use of black and more elaborate modesty coverings than other Delta provinces (see Chapter 6), and the Sa'idis by adopting the popular granny dress of the Delta with its full yoke, commodious, cuffed sleeves, trailing ruffle, and ankle-length skirt. Another marker of their relationship is found in the similarity between the speech of Sa'idis and many residents of Sharqiya who use the hard "G" sound instead of the "Q," and a soft "J" instead of a hard "G."[3]

NUBIANS

Photos[4] taken of Nubian women and children in 1868 show a very different dress than that worn today by Nubians. Lane, writing in the first half of the nineteenth century, describes the dress of women "in the Southern Province of Upper Egypt" as a large piece of dark-brown woolen material, called a *"Hulaleeyeh,"* which is wrapped around the body and then attached by the upper corners over each shoulder leaving the arms and most of the shoulders bare. A large piece of the same material is used as a tarha draped over the head. (Lane 1954, orig. 1860: 52–53) Photos of about this time show women wearing this coarse shapeless outfit while their children scamper around naked except for brief loincloths. Gordon writing in the 1860s says, "Up to 12 or 13, [Nubian girls] are neatly dressed in a bead necklace and a leather fringe four inches wide around the loins, and anything so absolutely perfect as their shapes or so sweetly innocent as their look can't be conceived" (1969 ed: 62). A half century before in Denon's drawings of Nubians during the Napoleonic expedition to Egypt, mature Nubian women

3. In the town of Bilbeis in Sharqiya for example several influences appear in the language of the inhabitants. Urban people speak with a Cairene accent, country people with a Sa'idi pattern and in the nearby desert, people speak in a characteristically bedouin way.
4. David D. Lorimer Bull, *Up the Nile: A Photographic Excursion: Egypt 1839–1898* (New York: Clarkson N. Potter, Inc., 1979).

were pictured in the scanty fringe and bead outfits that Gordon later wrote were reserved for immature girls.

In Nubia now the women are some of the most modestly dressed and most highly protected of all Egyptian women. There is considerable variation in the dress of Nubians (see Chapter 6 for modern variations) but two standard styles are the most prevalent,[5] characterizing the two main branches of Nubians, the Kenuz and the Fedija:

Kenuz

The basic dress of the Kenuz (originally the Northern Nubians living near Aswan) is most prominently characterized by vivid colors—reds, pinks, and oranges primarily, but also including the whole spectrum of rainbow colors. Dresses are usually made up in prints. The dress is ankle length and usually waisted with wide gathered sleeves. Tarhas similar in weave to the black shaal of Middle Upper Egypt may be in red, green, yellow, or pink, often with alternating zig-zag striped weaves. Lighter-weight tarhas of semi-transparent black or white materials are also common. The basic Kenuz dress is usually not covered by a modesty garment in the village other than the shoulder-enveloping shaal or tarha. In cities now, however, the Kenuz women may wear a standard yoked black modesty dress of a heavy material. A Kenzi male characterized the Kenuz as the most black-skinned of the Nubians, and the most "advanced." He insisted that most nowadays wear foreign dress but conceded that those in the surrounding villages still wear folk galabiyas.

Fedija

By contrast to the Kenuz, the dress of the Fedija (people originally from Southern Nubia) appears as a monotone of black. The typical outer modesty garment (the *jirjara*), which with the black heavy tarha is all the public observer sees, is a lightweight semi-transparent gauze georgette or net-like material, sometimes worked with a raised design of black flowers. It follows in general outlines the full granny dress. The jirjara has extremely wide sleeves, sometimes gathered loosely at the wrists, sometimes ending in a loose ruffle at the wrists. It is square-yoked at the neckline and falls to a long trailing *calash* (ruffle) adjusted by rows of horizontal tucks, in groups of three, near the middle of the skirt's length (characteristically in two groups, just below the knee, and at thigh level).

5. As one moves further south in Egypt, the Nubian dress comes more and more to resemble the sari-like garments of the Sudan.

Jirjara (also commonly found with tucks in groups of three at mid-thigh and just below the knee).

The outfit remains graceful and flowing because of the lightness of the material from which it is constructed. The over-all somber effect is partially relieved by the glimmer of color showing through the jirjara from the underdress below. This cotton basic dress is usually found in patterned prints. Mostly waisted styles are popular but occasionally a granny dress is observed. Until recently a large georgette tarha was embroidered with colored beads and tassels along its end edges and across the crown of the head on either side down over the shoulder, while a third piece intersected and fell down the center of the back.

Today many women embroider the black tarha with geometric patterns and flowers in thread, and some still wear chains with gold metal circular and triangular medallions from their foreheads and framing the sides of their faces. Necklaces, bracelets, and sometimes nose rings, all in heavy geometric shapes, complete the outfit of married women on festive occasions.

The dress of Sa'idi and Nubian, despite possible historical connections between them, reflects different ecological attachments. The Sa'idi is still primarily a farmer, who identifies most closely with Nile peasant dress as it is found in the Delta province of Sharqiya. As an Egyptian Arab he values property and working the land, and normally disdains the service industries the Nubians engage in. The Nubian on his side has a number of concerns and attachments: the protection of his women folk left at home, his more sophisticated knowledge of large areas of Egypt, his more extensive education, and his connections with Nubian tribal groups south of the border into the Sudan. All are reflected in one way or another in his own and his women's dress. His dress can afford to be distinctive if for no reason than that any kind of dress cannot conceal the physical features that make him visibly Nubian. On top of this negative reason is also the positive one that Nubians possess a strong ethos of pride in their community's superiority and their own cleanliness, honesty, and industriousness.

A final dress description, this one of a Nubian dress found in the Cairo Folkloric Museum, ends the section on Nubians. This dress is interesting because it may provide a link between Nubian dress and the dress found in the Kharga-to-Bahriya complex of oases described below, and even possibly to the dress of the far western oasis of Siwa. In the Museum, which tends to display costumes of several decades ago, it is simply marked "Nubian Thawb," with no further markers of origin.

The dress is cut similarly to a bedouin pattern, with center and back panels, side panels from under the arms and reaching to the hem, and arm pieces that fill in the upper bodice and reach to the wrists in a single piece. The material is a heavy black cotton. The neckline is oval with a second narrow oval providing an extended slit for taking the dress on and off more easily. The neckline proper is outlined with small buttons and the rest of the dress decoration is composed of running stitches and filled areas in purple, yellow, and blue threads. This decorative work outlines the neckline slit oval, forms a deep rounded V-shape from shoulder to center front, and forms several streamers from the lower edge of the neck slit, one vertical (and intersecting the V-point) and two at 45 degree angles pointing to either side. At the end of these two streamers, two more streamers point down to parallel and equal the center streamer. Each streamer ends in an oval with groups of three sunburst stitches completing the design. The overall effect is simple with accents on the front bodice with its conspicuous medallion pattern and the streamers emanating from it. Except for its decorative embroidery the dress is very similar to the tawb found in Isna (see Chapter 3). The embroidery resembles the sunburst pattern found in Siwa oasis.

Physical characteristics of some of the oasis peoples suggest a past association with Nubian groups, and if this were not enough to have influenced their dress styles, both peoples had a strong connection with the caravan trade that ran north and south between Egypt and the Sudan.

THE OASES

The three major oases complexes of Egypt: the Fayoum, Kharga and its circle of smaller oases, and Siwa, are about as unalike in their circumstances as they are in their dress. Each clings in one way or another to different life-line connections with the outside world. In many ways oasis communities become discretely defined by their environmentally induced separation from other communities and the character of their intermittent links. The desert allows for no gradual transitions.

The Fayoum

Pharoahs in the 12th dynasty (about 2000 B.C.) constructed the *Bahr Youssef* (Joseph's Canal) which forks off of a canal north of Assyut and enters the Fayoum along the present-day road to Beni Suef. The canals radiating out through the oases from the Bahr Youssef, coupled with the large collecting basin of Lake Qarun, make it possible to cultivate wide areas of fruit trees, olives, and field crops. The people of Fayoum are primarily farmers engaged in agriculture and concerned with the markets where those crops can be sold. A small number of bedouin however also have attached themselves to the oases where they can easily water their flocks or engage in trade between Fayoum and other oases, like Bahriya. Craftsmen such as carpenters, silver makers, and metal workers make up a third important part of the oasis economy.

The closest major city to Fayoum now, as in the past, is Beni Suef which is little more than a third the distance of Cairo on the present asphalted road. The dress of the majority of the inhabitants of Fayoum is a peasant dress with no pretense at desert or other unique identity. As noted above (see Chapter 3), the dress closely resembles that of Beni Suef and towns like Bayad across on the east side of the Nile. The dress is a waisted style reaching to a little below the knee. The sleeves are full. A fitted band separates the waist from the breasts which are often outlined underneath with contrasting braid. In some dresses a shirred front piece indicates the separation of the breasts and is continued along the neckline by the two lapels of a collar or material artificially marked with braid to resemble a collar. The dress is usually of solid-colored heavy cotton, topped with a heavy shawl (usually black) as a modesty covering. Older women usually wear black dresses, while younger women wear bright colors.

The Fayoum dress bears no resemblance to the Delta granny dress whose influence extends down to an area very near to the connection of a secondary road from the upper Fayoum and the major north-south road along the Nile. Within a radius of 20 kilometers of this road connection a virtual battle of the granny and waisted styles goes on (see Chapter 8).

Kharga, Dakhla, Farafra, Bahriya

The oases connected by road to the Nile Valley, on the Kharga side with Assyut, and the Bahriya side with Cairo, differ considerably in scenic advantages but share a similar environmental adjustment. Though each oasis in some ways is unique, culturally Kharga and Dakhla form a similar unit and Farafra and Bahriya another. However, all their dresses share enough common themes to confirm a more general connection.

People in these oases call themselves neither bedouin nor fellahin, meaning in this case that they feel they are a people with a separate identity. The facial features of many of them have a characteristic appearance that is easily recognized. A talented local potter in Kharga who satirizes activities of the inhabitants exaggerates the faces of his little figurines to accentuate the oasis features. These can best be described as a somewhat bulging lower cheek area, as though the person perpetually had a mouth full of food or was blowing on a balloon. Other oasis inhabitants have appearances that range from the narrow fine features of the bedouin to the negroid features of Nubia. The separate identity of the oasis was not, perhaps, always so separate.

Kharga

Kharga, the largest oasis of the crescent, includes a number of villages that huddle around their respective wells and are separated by encroaching sands. Conditions tend to be difficult and agriculture often precarious. Strong winds sweep across the oasis depression, wells fill with sand, water dries up in one area

Fayoum Oasis.   Bayad Village.

and must be sought at deeper levels or in new locations. With recent government irrigation projects, water has become more dependable. But the projects have brought government workers and government officials from all over Egypt to live and mingle with the local populations. This influence coupled with improved road and rail links, and migration of the young men to the Nile Valley in search of work, have all contributed to breaking down the isolation of the oases. Now many young men expect to migrate for part of their working careers to earn the additional incomes necessary to acquire the goods people have become used to. As the social gulf between the Nile Valley and the oasis narrows, it becomes difficult with casual observation to detect a difference in dress or other superficial behavior between the two areas. In the oasis it has become a mark of sophistication to dress and carry on a life style like the people of the Valley. People in the towns of the oases now wear foreign dress and granny and waisted styles of folk dress from diverse regions of origin. The true oases' dresses are seen only in small villages on older women or at special occasions. Nevertheless the change is recent enough so that dress identifiably from one oasis or another still bears strong traces in the memory of most inhabitants.

The distinctive dress that is associated with Kharga oasis, as in other oases, differs somewhat from individual dress to dress and from village to village without losing its basic similarity of style. Early twentieth-century versions of the dress show more extensive embroidery than present-day versions yet the same similarity persists. The basic black dress on which the embroidery is found remains virtually the same for all the oases and is very much like the dress of the Egyptian bedouin in style and cut. It differs considerably from either the waisted or the granny dress of the Nile Valley.

The dress is a wide A-line from shoulder to hem, (slightly narrowed at the waist) with oval neckline and often an extended slit of several inches in the center front. The sleeves of the oases dwellers are consistently straight, long to the wrist and narrow, while bedouin dress sleeves show much greater variety. The dress material itself varies from heavy muslins to heavy cottons, or sateens, and is always black, possibly for practical reasons as well as to show up the distinctive embroidery.

Oasis embroidery differs from bedouin embroidery by its use of an assortment of stitches from running stitches to cross stitch. It is a primitive kind of crewel work in contrast to the fine and invariable cross stitch of the bedouin. In Kharga that embroidery is distinctive for its central panel of thin vertical embroidered stripes that may or may not have parallel lines of small geometric squares arranged in clusters in-between. An early twentieth-century dress extended these vertical lines crossed by horizontal lines from neck to hem, broken into four horizontal rectangular sub-panels. A recent dress extended vertical lines to the hem but extended the inter-spatial geometric patterns only half way down the dress. The side seams are also marked by thin lines of embroidery from underarm to hem.

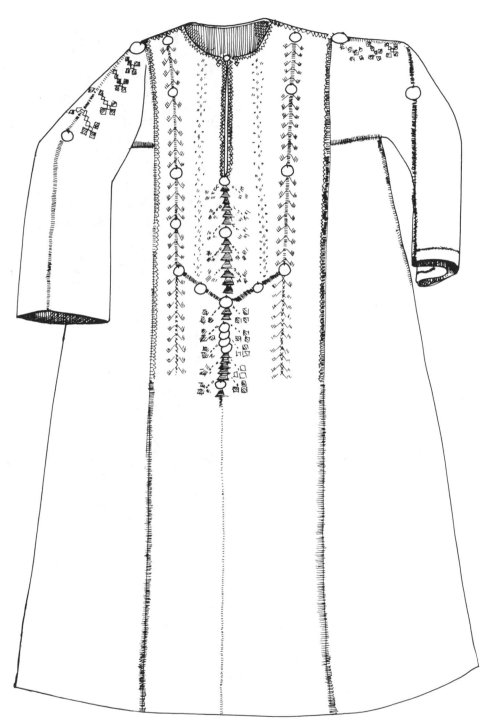

Kharga dress (modern, simplified).

Dakhla dress (village of Allamun).

All the embroidery in the Kharga dress is the same color of faded rosy red, probably a few shades lighter than the original color. In equidistant spacings, silver coins are joined to the dress along the main vertical lines and extend, in the modern dress, beyond the more extensively worked panel to the hem. The effect of the embroidered parts of the Kharga dress is of an overall sameness of evenly spaced decorative motifs and coins. In the dress as a whole the center front panel is accentuated but only mildly when compared with the focal point it creates in dresses from other oases.

Detail of Dakhla dress
(Allamun).

Dakhla

Kharga's collection of villages is neighbored most closely by its beautiful
sister oasis, Dakhla, which itself is composed of a number of small villages. Between villages, the dresses of Dakhla vary, but still retain enough similarity to
show their connection. Two specimens will give an idea of both the variations
and constants.

The basic black dress of Dakhla remains essentially the same as Kharga,
with decorative contrasts still predominantly red embroidery and silver coins. The
Allamun dress has accentuating lines of embroidery mainly in reds, but yellows
and pale blue are compacted together to give heavy and more prominent out-

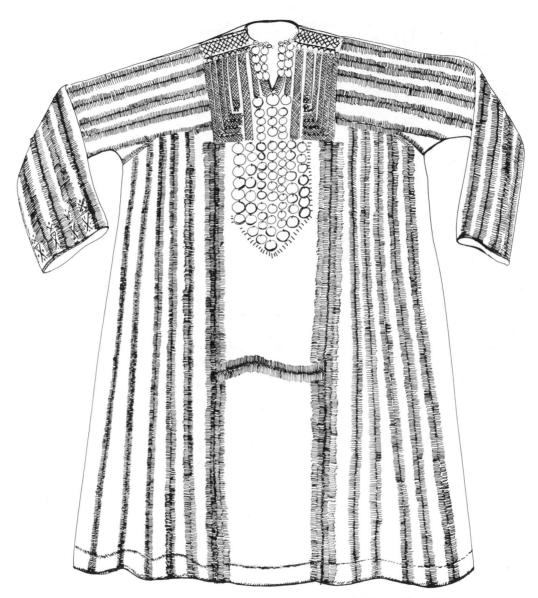

Dakhla Oasis (Ballot village, style 1).

line to the central design, a rectangular front panel elongating to a point just below the waist. Small rectangular insets from the shoulder down to the bust, and separated by the neck slit that is embroidered and extended below the opening, make up the first part of the panel; the second half consists of three heavy lines of a squared V-shape, one inside another. As often happens in oasis dress,

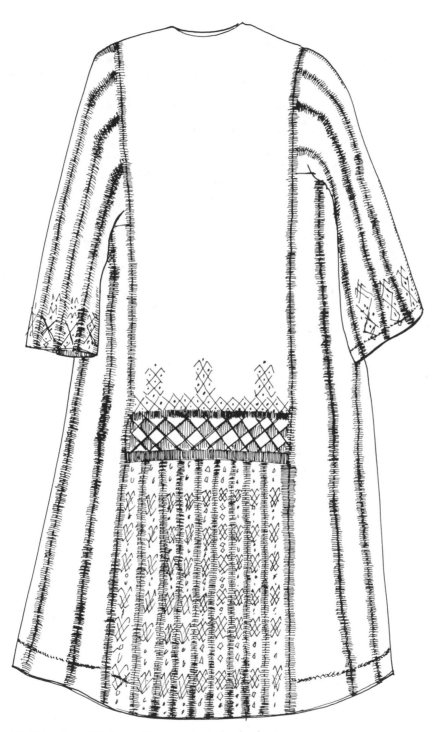

Dakhla Oasis (Ballot village, style 1, back view).

Detail of Dakhla dress (Ballot transitional style).

coins indicate the points of emphasis,— in this case accentuating the small rectangular squares, neck slit, and V-shaped rows of embroidery. The overall effect is one of a large single medallion shape covering the whole upper torso area.

One variety of dress in Ballot village has much more extensive embroidery than the Allamun dress, in some respects a negative image of the Kharga dress, with stripes of heavy red lines enclosing an orange-yellow line extending both the length of the dress on either side under the arms and also the length of the sleeve. The center front panel, so important in the Kharga dress, is left empty below the waist in the Ballot dress as it is in the Allamun dress.

Heavy embroidery, almost obscuring the dress material in reds and pale blues, forms a square yoke at the neck and more heavy embroidery in somewhat large patterns of the same colors plus orange-yellow fill in the bottom center panel at the back. This is more reminiscent of the areas covered by embroidery in bedouin dress. Were it only for the embroidery, the Ballot dress would bear little more than a general resemblance to the Allamun dress, but as in the latter, coins again serve to point out the distinguishing feature. Heavy lines of closely spaced coins extend the neck slit, outline the yoke and form a heavy medallion similar to the Allamun dress. This medallion is reminiscent of the silver inset found in

Detail of Dakhla dress
(Ballot).

the Harrah dress and may therefore also take its inspiration from the *telly* work
found in the Nile valley.

A second style of Ballot dress bears less resemblance to the Allamun dress
but provides a transitional style to those dresses found in the western oasis of
Farafra and Bahriya. In this dress the underarm and sleeve stripes are wider, there
is no neck front opening, and the elongated front medallion is gone. The square
yoke is outlined by small white buttons (replacing the coins) across the shoulder,
around the neck, and zigzaging along the lower edge of the vertical lines making
up the pattern of the yoke. Another line of buttons outlines horizontal stripes
on the lowest part of the yoke and coins closely draw a final horizontal accent.

As a modesty garment a large heavy black futa or *ghatra* (head cloth) is worn

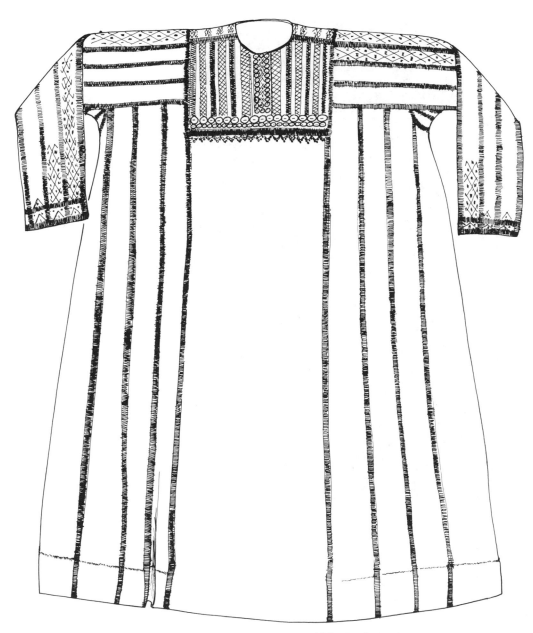

Dakhla Oasis (Ballot village, style 2).

over the head and pulled around the shoulder like a cloak. The edges are embroidered in red with a double row pattern of filled-in zig-zags. For decorative
effect a subtly striped silk kerchief with tassels is worn under and partly concealed

Dakhla: *futa,* head scarf, and face veil, worn until recently in the oasis but
now no longer seen as a complete outfit except possibly on older women.

by the futa, appearing as a frame for the forehead. On the scarf are sewn a row
of coins to frame the face. Coins and buttons are also found frequently used by
bedouins in the decoration of face masks and head cloths in the Hijaz regions
of Saudi Arabia.

Farafra

Across a large expanse of desert to the northwest of Dakhla lies what has
historically been the poorest and most isolated of the oases, Farafra. The recent

asphalting of roads connecting Farafra with Dakhla and Bahriya, and numerous government development projects including the drilling of wells that bring employment and ample water, have brought a prosperity to Farafra greater than before. Except for the road routes mentioned above that mediate contact with the outside world through other oases, the only other direct connection link Farafra has had is with distant Siwa oasis by desert track. Caravans, however, coming from Siwa often bypassed Farafra by taking shorter routes to Minya and points north.

Compared with the people of Dakhla and Bahriya, the Farafronis speak a distinctly different dialect. Fakhry claims they have more bedouin Arab blood in their veins and are less negroid in feature than many from Bahriya (1974: 170–71). In this respect it is interesting that Farafra is the only one of the four oases where camels can be raised because it lacks the insects that cause a serious camel disease. Despite these differences, Farafra and Bahriya share cultural traits, according to Fakhry.

The dress the Farafra style most closely resembles is that of the South Sinai bedouin. Both possess the same major characteristics: the black bedouin foundation dress, a hem ruffle, and an emphasis on the embroidery of the sleeve. With its yoke and ruffle, it also resembles certain of the Delta granny styles.[6] As in the other oases, this "typical" dress is becoming more and more difficult to see, except as worn by older women.

The basic Farafra dress falls to the ankles in gathers from a separate sewn-on square yoke piece. In mature women the gathers may be modified to open pleats. The sleeves are gathered and cuffed instead of straight and uncuffed as in other oases' dresses, but like those dresses the bodice and sleeve are a single piece not joined by a seam. The parts of the dress below the yoke may fall to the ankles unadorned or there may be a short ruffle circling the hem edge (again similar to many Delta dresses).

The neckline is oval and opens with a slit opening in the back. Both neckline and yoke edge are outlined in red piping, the latter also including a red zig-zag line in the bodice front to accentuate the edge. What makes it immediately recognizable as an oasis dress is the row of silver coins that outline the yoke front and back. Bahriya women said that the dress of Farafra was distinctive because of the "worked piece on the sleeve and because of the ruffle," but I have not been able to determine what the worked piece on the sleeve was. Nowadays women mostly wear waisted or granny cotton dresses with a shawl to cover their heads. Popular at the time I visited was a red, white, and blue woven zig-zag striped shawl. Farafronis are reputed to be more religious than their neighbors, their women rarely seen, and they are said to care little for personal adornment (Fakhry 1974:172).

6. Until recently Farafra's closest relations were with the inhabitants of Bahriya which not only

Bahriya

North east of Farafra lies the far-flung oasis of Bahriya with its major town al-Bawiti. Most of the major villages of Bahriya lie along an east-west axis oriented by the scattered wells that still sustain the villages but which once served as a major caravan route from the Siwa Oasis to the Nile Valley towns of Bani Mazar, and Samalut near Minya (the route is called Bahnasa). The north-south (actually north-east by south-west) axis of Bahriya is the present major route, now asphalted through Bahriya, and serving traffic to Cairo to the north and Farafra to the south. Bawiti town is located at the crossroads of these two major routes, old and new.

The inhabitants of Bahriya come from a variety of origins: the original inhabitants of the oasis, migrants from Dakhla oasis, bedouin coming from the coastal areas of the Western Desert, and Upper Egyptians coming mainly from the areas around Minya. The inhabitants of the village of al-Aguuz are from the Siwa oasis, the women banished, according to historical texts, for their immoral behavior (Fakhry 1974:21–22, 38–39). Fakhry comments that the peoples of Bahriya have mixed to such an extent that except for small details in the dress that can be traced to outside origins, there is little to indicate the original diversity of their origins.

As is the case in other oases, there is some variety in the decorative patterns of dresses at the same time that there are elements which give a distinctive Bahriya flavor to a particular outfit. On the basic black dress, it is characteristic in Bahriya to leave the lower front center panel undecorated. Side panels and sleeves are worked in reds and pale yellows with wide vertical stripes composed of lines and triangles. Similar but horizontal lines below the knee give the appearance of a large ruffle at the hem line.

What is most characteristic of the Bahriya dress is the heavily worked elements of the bodice which at the lower edges and at the shoulders is accented with rows of red tassels. The worked parts consist of three heavily embroidered rectangles, two covering the bodice at right and left under the shoulder, and the third centered between them and lower. Coins outline the rectangles, extend the neckline slit, and a second row of coins accents the lower edge of the center rectangle.

As a modesty wrap, the large rectangular subtly colored (black, rose, and white) plaid wool futa (a collective term used for a piece of cloth) is often employed, the one that is found in old Nile Valley caravan towns like Qena and called nishra there. It is made in Nagada, a town north of Luxor. Others wear a red or plain black futa with modest zig-zag braid around the edges. In summer

---

was nearer, but where Farafonis regularly received their mail. Now Farafra has been administratively tied to Dakhla, and with the new road links, travel has become easier in both directions.

Bahriya dress; often the dress has tassels at the shoulders.

the tarha may be worn alone or in winter under the futa. A person dressed in the classical costume is not fully dressed without a gold nostril decoration.

Until 1971 Bahriya's significant link with the Nile Valley was recognized by its administrative inclusion as part of the governorate of Minya. It was from Minya that the mail came over the Bahnasa route to the town of Harrah, the first stop on the edge of the oasis, where eager officials from Bahwiti saved a day's time by riding out to await the mail bag (Fakhry 1974:25). It is interesting to note that at this mail stop, Harrah, a special dress is seen until this day. In most ways similar to other Bahriya dresses, it is strikingly different in the center rectangular piece, which has been substituted with a pear-shaped piece of Nile Valley *tull bi telly* work. Telly consists of silver threads embroidered on a fine net-like

Detail of Bahriya dress.

tulle, and, is rarely found now in use. Telly is associated with elaborate full-length dresses worn by elite urban women in Assyut many decades ago. The telly pieces used in the Harrah dresses are only small insets but their elegance and the fineness of the materials used contrast sharply with the coarseness of the other materials used in the basic oasis dress. In the women's minds there was perhaps an association of the silver embroidery with the silver coins so prominently used in providing accents in oasis dresses.

One last decorative item that was prominent in Bahriya until recently, when gold replaced it in the esteem of the natives, was silver jewelry. The silver work was bought from traders of Fayoum who specialized in silver work for oasis and bedouin women. One characteristic piece, a large circular medallion with small silver balls attached to the sides and bottom, had etched in its face a crude stick figure representing the folk hero, Abu-Zeid al Hilali.

A similar thread of inspiration thus runs through the dresses of the several oases of the Kharga complex, uniting them and making them recognizable as possessing a common root source. They stand out as distinctive from Nile Valley and bedouin dress.

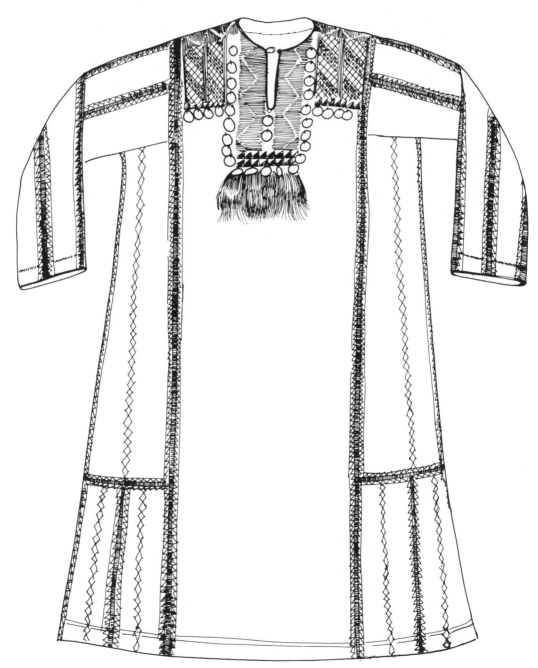

Bahriya Oasis (also frequently found with shoulder tassels).

Women of the oasis: younger in yoked modern style; older in Harrah dress
with *telly* inset.

Siwa

Siwa oasis, by its geographic position, has had more historical connections
with Libya than with Egypt proper. This connection is reflected in the greater
use of a North African Berber dialect by the inhabitants than their second lan-

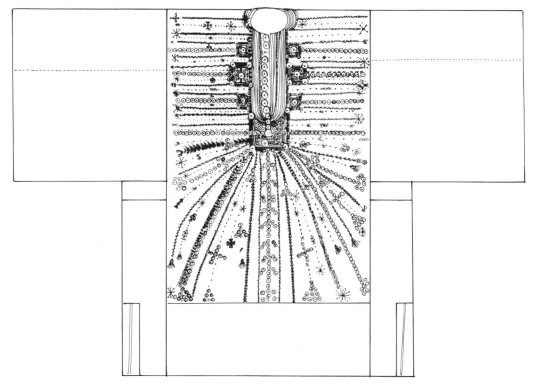

Siwa Oasis tunic.

guage, Arabic. Until recently Siwa was accessible only by caravan or desert vehicle over long and difficult desert tracks from Libya, Mersa Matruh, Bahriya, and Kirdasa. Now, an asphalted three-hundred-kilometer road from Mersa Matruh (the old Darb al-Mahashas route) and the increasing importance of the oasis as a military outpost in the defense against Libya has increased the frequency and duration of contacts with outsiders, principally with Egyptians.

When compared with the larger oases of Kharga, Dakhla, Bahriya, and Fayoum, Siwa's population is small.[7] Its principal economic activity is the cultivation of dates, which has been historically accomplished through a complicated

7. In 1976 the population of Siwa was 6,887. The larger oases of Kharga, Dakhla, Bahriya, and Fayoum have, according to the same census, populations of 38,519; 46,656; 14,177; and 166,910 (Fayoum city only) respectively. Farafra is by far the smallest oasis with only 1515 inhabitants. It is also the poorest in terms of natural resources.

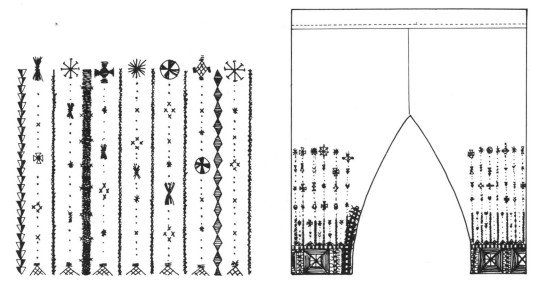

Siwa Oasis: Women's under trousers, right figure; head covering (detail), left figure.

system of hired, unmarried laborers who with the native residents form a caste system in the oasis.

Siwan women are among the most protected of all Egyptian women and are rarely seen outside the privacy of their homes. If a woman is glimpsed by a visitor, it is usually as a black shadow slipping from house to house; there is little opportunity to observe the true beauty of the traditional costume of the oasis.

Fakhry, describing the Siwan costume in 1938 when he first visited the oasis, says:

The young girls who play in the streets are dressed in garments of very bright colors with wide, long sleeves and they wear around their necks bead necklaces. . . . It is a source of pride to every woman to have her hair done in many small, thin tresses, numbering as many as 30 or 40, and to do the hair of any of her daughters who have reached the age of eleven or twelve in the same way. . . . Whenever the women . . . go out to attend a marriage . . . or to make any important visit they might well wear more than one garment. However, the outside robe must be black in color with rich silk embroidery of variegated colors around the neck and the front part of the dress, and they must wear a number of their traditional silver ornaments. . . . In their houses,

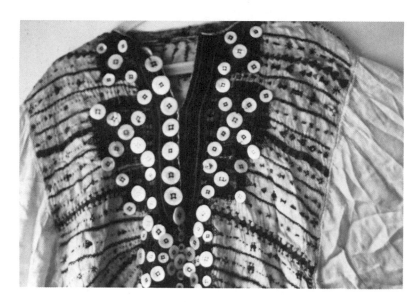

Detail of Siwa dress: sunburst design.

the women wear garments of bright colors, always with wide, long sleeves.
. . . When they go out, they . . . put on trousers of white cotton cloth tight
at the ankles, the lower parts embroidered with colored silk in beautiful geometric designs. Whenever a Siwan woman leaves her house she wraps herself
in a wide sheet of cloth (called a *milayah*), striped in black and gray. It is
. . . always imported from the village of Kirdasah, near the pyramids of Giza
where for hundreds of years some of the families have woven this kind of cloth
for the Siwans. Kirdasah was the starting point of all the caravans which used
to travel between Cairo and Siwa up to the 20s of this century. Whenever
the women see a stranger they pull the milayah together over their faces, leaving only a small hole for one or both eyes, since they never use veils (Fakhry
1973:45, 47).

Now, children dress much like children of other areas of Egypt. During the
school year their standard dress is the school uniform obligatory in most areas
of the country. Women wear colored cotton dresses in their homes, reserving for
special occasions the elaborate embroidered traditional costumes. As in other areas
of Egypt, it is the older women who make the most frequent use of traditional
dress.

The dress characteristic of Siwa is unique in Egypt. Most commonly it is
made up in preparation for marriage either in black or white silk or white cotton.
The basic dress, formed like a huge "T," is extremely wide and bears little rela-

Shoes worn in Siwa oasis.

tion to the wearer's dimensions. The "shoulder" seam droops almost to the elbow and the sleeves fall in folds that are difficult to distinguish from the body of the dress. The garment is composed of large rectangular and square pieces of material combined in such a way that smaller pieces form the underarms and sides.

It is only in the leggings that the material is tapered at the ankle and lower leg from a wide gathered waist and baggy crotch. From mid-calf to ankle this legging is visible, exposing an intricate embroidery that matches the central embroidered panel of the dress. The rich multi-colored (reds, oranges, yellows, blues, and greens) silk embroidery with accenting rows of small circular mother-of-pearl buttons, radiate out in sunburst rays from an elongated neckline opening. Some observers suggest that the sunburst design is a throwback to sun-worshipping rituals of an early period, and the contemporary buttons a substitution for the mother-of-pearl that was acquired from a trade in shells with coastal areas. The silk embroidery radiating out from the center portions uses different types of stitching, much like modern crewel work, to define the sunlike rays. Often midway and at the extremities of rays, a special spokelike pattern gives the illusion of the sparkle in sunlight. With the added light that catches in the shiny buttons, the design, in effect, captures both the rainbow of colors and brightness of real sunlight.

The Siwan costume has its closest correlates, as far as the shape of the dress is concerned, in some North African apparel, notably in costumes of earlier periods in Tunisia. The occasional use of mother-of-pearl buttons and frequent use

Siwan modesty wrap.

of similar decorative stitching in oases of the Kharga complex attest to a close and regular contact maintained by the caravans of the Western Desert. One such contact has already been mentioned in the "immoral women" of Siwa who were banished, according to the historical record, to villages in the Bahriya oasis. In many ways Siwan dress is a good illustration of how elements in dress can reflect the myriad attachments of a particular community while at the same time preserving a uniqueness to the whole costume that sets the community apart from others.

Desert and Coastal Dwellers

✦5

"Walk hungry before your enemy but not naked"—Arab proverb[1]

ANOTHER WAY OF LIFE exists in Egypt, in addition to that of the Nile Valley and the oases, where lives stabilize around sweet-water sources and small cultivatable plots of land. Subsistence depends mainly on the mobility of humans exploiting natural resources extensively rather than intensively. The bedouin compose one such group and the fisher people of the coastal plain another. Both may or may not reside in fairly fixed locations, but their livelihood is sought in far-flung directions, in desert grazing, in long-distance transport of goods (by camel or modern truck), or by seeking out the best harvest of fish along coastal waterways in shallow water traps and deep sea netting.

BEDOUIN

Bedouin dress patterns are extremely complicated and do not lend themselves easily to neat categorization. This, in itself, reveals something about the contemporary nomadic scene. Now, many of the bedouin settle either permanently or during a good part of the year in towns along the northern coast of Egypt proper and the Sinai, near oases, and in cultivated areas along the Nile. They fill niches in agricultural communities where, with their camels, they help bring in crops like sugar cane; in return, or for a fee, they obtain grazing rights for their sheep on what remains of harvested lands.

Even in Sharqiya governorate where they are well established, the bedouin tend to lead separate lives from those of local agriculturalists. At the same time, they have adjusted in varying degrees to sending their children to school and to living in more permanent structures, sometimes alongside bedouin of other tribal

1. This proverb means "Do not show your weakness."

77

groups. Today there are fewer identifiable markers that define the divisions between tribal segments. What seems most important for bedouin to preserve is
the larger distinction between themselves, peasants, oasis people, and other groups
in Egyptian society. In this effort their dress serves as a distinguishing feature.

Even so, bedouin maintain that there still exist a number of markers in dress
that convey subtle and specific meanings. The fact that these distinctions are not
consistently observable to an outsider does not erase from the minds of the bedouin themselves the conviction that markers of significance exist. In all probability these markers with their implications persist as one of several frames of
reference, understood when they appear but not invariably required by tribal
members.

This section will give, first, general information on the elements and construction of bedouin dress. Then it will describe the dress of the bedouin of north
and south Sinai, and the Mediterranean and Red Sea Coasts to illustrate some
of the range of variation and the way bedouin themselves manipulate the elements of dress.

The foundation dress that provides background for the decorative detail of
the bedouin is made of heavy black cotton, poplin, or sateen material. Black is
practical in not showing dirt; it can be bought by the bolt for use as the need
arises and one shade of black does not vary much from another, so older dresses
can be patched conveniently to prolong their wear. The basic dress comes in a
loose-fitting straight A-line style (not gathered by a yoke as in the peasant granny
style). Sleeves either form narrow elongated cylinders with no cuffs, or flare in
triangular cones to the wrists. This last "princess" style sleeve is called *burdan*.

If styles of clothing were ranked by level of sophistication in dressmaking
construction, the bedouin dress would rank as an ancient survival. The word for
the dress, tawb, means literally a bolt of material and, true to its name, its construction relies at least as heavily on the dimensions of the material it uses as
it does on the shape of the figure it covers. This is convenient because such a
construction wastes barely a scrap of material and allows the finished selvages
maximal use so seam edges do not fray. All pieces are geometrical in shape and
all have their opposing number so that a "right" triangle cut out of the rectangular bolt for a sleeve produces a reverse "right" triangle for the second sleeve. It
is only at the neckline that a small oval must be cut out of these otherwise per-
fectly straight geometric sets.

The illustration on page 83 shows how a dress pattern is cut out of two different width sizes of material. In Egypt, at present, material is bought primarily
in three widths, ard (36 inches or 90 centimeters) or ard w nuss (45 inches or
about 115–120 centimeters) and ardeen (about 140 centimeters). It is still most
common to find materials used for folk dress in the narrower 90–100 centimeter
width. This was traditionally the standard width of hand looms.

From the pattern layouts it is clear that dress can be made more efficiently with less wastage of material out of the same yardage of narrow (90 centimeter) material as a wider material. It is quite likely that many dimensions of bedouin dress are arbitrary, designed to use up extra pieces in between pattern pieces. The sleeve in particular can assume a number of shapes—cylindrical, conical (wider at the wrist or narrower at the wrist)—varying partly according to style and partly according to availability of material. It is not unusual to find an irregular piece, as for example a slightly squared off "H" piece (see diagram), used to take up the small extra piece of material between "H" and "C." Or if piece "A" or "B" is not long enough, another scrap may be added on to fill the gap.

In general now, sleeves are most often straight cylinders and fairly narrow (like those of a Western suit jacket). Bedouin say that the exaggerated conical style sleeve (burdan) is no longer practical: cold air rushes up the sleeve in winter, its ends have to be tied behind the wearer to prevent them getting tangled in activities, and modesty now requires that a woman wear another tight-fitting sleeve under the tawb to cover her bare arms. What was once considered the convenience of a well-ventilated garment has been replaced by the requisites of modesty.

The modesty argument is probably a recent one. Not only the aspect of less revealing sleeves but the heavy veiling of many contemporary bedouin women, by some reports, did not exist in the last century. Lucy Duff Gordon writing in the 1860s was surprised by the "immodesty" (in Egyptian terms) of the bedouin women. One bedouin she described as wearing "a white sack cloth and veil[2] and nothing else." This woman, on a journey alone, shook hands with Gordon "with the air of a princess . . . and strode off across the graveyard like a stately ghost." (1969 ed.:47). In another instance Gordon describes a young bedouin woman, "dressed like a man" who appeared "unabashed but not impudent or swaggering" who enjoyed the company of men and travel. She wandered alone with her own camel, remained a virgin and rejected the idea of marriage (1969 ed.:110). In a final comment, Gordon sums up her observations on the bedouin, "To see a Bedouin and his wife walk through the streets of Cairo is superb. Her hand resting on his shoulder and scarcely deigning to cover her haughty face. She looks down on the Egyptian veiled woman who carries the heavy burden and walks behind her lord and master" (1969 ed.:77).

It would not be the first time that elements of dress like veiling passed from an urban part of the population to a rural one, becoming lost in the meantime to the urban groups. Nubian dress in the same period also became much more concerned with modesty as we have seen.

Though modesty and bolt dimensions have their impact on dress styles, none would survive were they not in some way suitable for the environment in which

2. Gordon often refers to the head cloth as a veil and this may be what she means here. By her tone she feels something was missing and her comment later suggests that the bedouin woman holds her head cloth across part of her face rather than wearing a full veil.

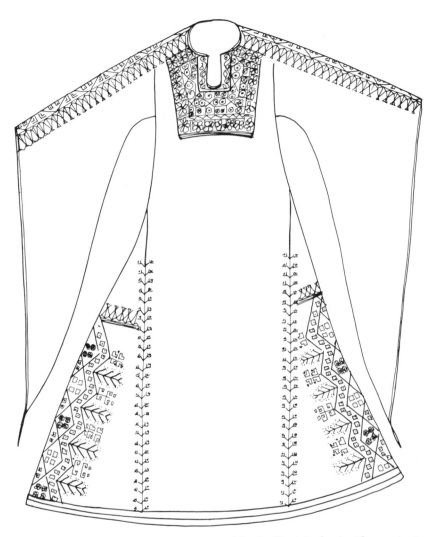

North Sinai Bedouin (front view).

the bedouin are forced to survive. The loose-flowing, many-layered outfits create both ventilation currents and insulation from extremes of hot and cold as needed. They are comfortable for riding camels or donkeys, tending sheep, and for other necessary functions.

As mentioned earlier black surfaces absorb heat, but with intermediate layers underneath they do not create temperatures that are any warmer for the wearer than white surfaces. The head is also usually covered with more than one layer that not only protects from the elements but accomplishes the vital purpose for

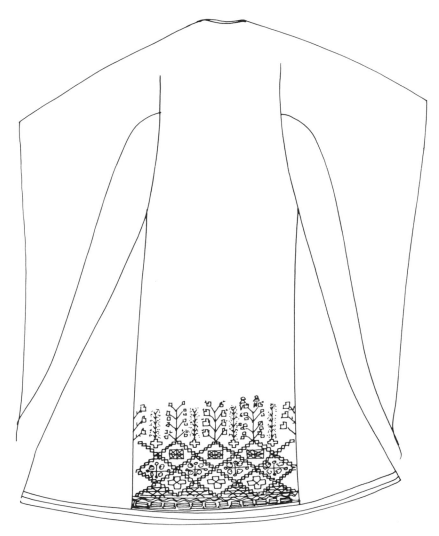

North Sinai Bedouin (back view).

bedouin, as for peasants, of keeping head lice down and the hair protected from dirt. For men and women the side corners of the headdress are often piled on top of the head to provide cooling shade while the currents of air move freely around the wearer's neck. In winter the wearer can wrap them tightly around the face to protect from the cold.

It is characteristic to see bedouin women tie their lighter-weight head scarves (including tarha-like scarves) in a knot at the back of the head on the level of the ears, rather than crossing the ends at the back base of the neck and tying the knot just over the forehead as most peasants do. This accomplishes the same cooling effect while leaving the back of the neck shaded. It also serves to keep a woman's headgear firmly battened down in a wind.

Summer and winter, bedouin fight the sweeping ravages of desert winds that dry and toughen the skin and resist their attempts to move against its force. Enveloping clothing on the one hand protects against the drying effect and the cold while on the other hampering movements much in the way the sail of a boat requires tacking to make headway against a wind. It is not unreasonable to speculate that the numerous ways bedouin devise to tie themselves together owe something to this problem. The woman ties her head scarf down in the distinctive way described above and binds her middle in the stomach region with a wide band that reduces her bulk and holds in the heat in winter. Her face veil is anchored with rows of heavy coins.

The man almost invariably wears an *agal* (head rope) whose origin is said to have been for the equally binding use of hobbling animals. It helps keep his side vision free, and along with his head scarf can be used for tying bundles of goods, or restraining animals. The head scarf (*kafiya*) of the bedouin hangs loosely over his shoulders, is white and light-weight in summer, and red-and-white, or black-and-white check heavier-weight cotton in the winter. In the heat he may pile the ends of the cloth carelessly on top of his head. The peasant by contrast wraps his head several times with his head scarf in a haphazard way that needs constant adjustment, and without any kind of head band proves vulnerable in a wind. Most bedouin wear some kind of belt at the waist—a rope, or a thick leather belt with compartments for necessities. The peasant, wearing a similar dress, allows his robe to flap in the wind. The distance he traverses from house to fields is short and the looseness of his garment cools him after his hard work. In the fields, the peasant works in his underwear or tucks his galabiya around his waist to free his movements. It is the belt, a recognizable head scarf, and the agal headband that are the most immediate signals for distinguishing the bedouin male from townspeople or peasants.

The bright-colored embroideries of the bedouin women's dress may similarly have adaptive qualities as well as being aesthetically pleasing to a people who live in a mostly beige and grey world. The colors are visible for long distances which immediately makes it possible to distinguish people from the landscape. When the colors come in distinctive patterns that distinguish tribal segments, they reveal whether a woman sheep-herder or water-carrier should or should not be approached, a social but also a territorial convenience that may prevent conflicts. Women's place in the tribe was always a protected one, understood mutually even by bitter enemies to be inviolable. Men's clothing is more subdued and blends more successfully into the scenery. As protectors and potential competitors they are better served by avoiding the high profile of a conspicuous costume.

The brightly colored sashes worn bound around their waists and tied in back

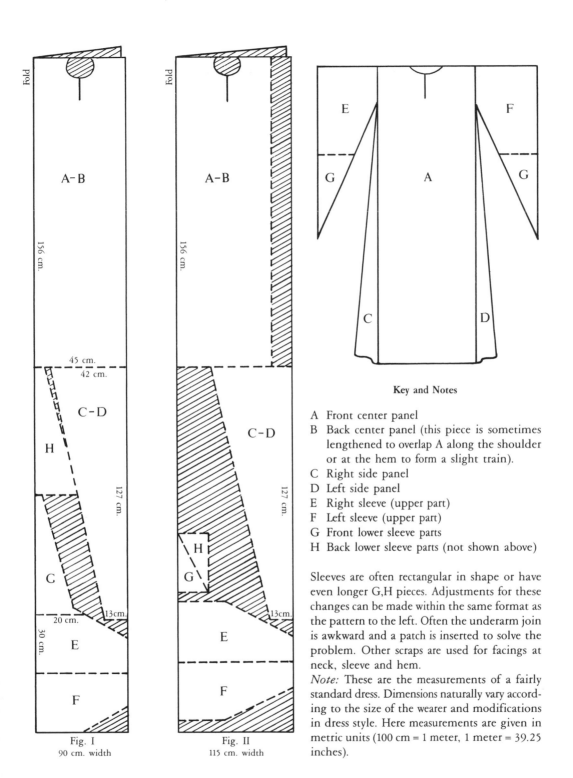

Key and Notes

A Front center panel
B Back center panel (this piece is sometimes lengthened to overlap A along the shoulder or at the hem to form a slight train).
C Right side panel
D Left side panel
E Right sleeve (upper part)
F Left sleeve (upper part)
G Front lower sleeve parts
H Back lower sleeve parts (not shown above)

Sleeves are often rectangular in shape or have even longer G,H pieces. Adjustments for these changes can be made within the same format as the pattern to the left. Often the underarm join is awkward and a patch is inserted to solve the problem. Other scraps are used for facings at neck, sleeve and hem.

Note: These are the measurements of a fairly standard dress. Dimensions naturally vary according to the size of the wearer and modifications in dress style. Here measurements are given in metric units (100 cm = 1 meter, 1 meter = 39.25 inches).

Fig. I
90 cm. width

Fig. II
115 cm. width

Material Requirements for Bedouin Dresses

are also the most reliable sign of a woman's bedouin identity in Egypt. Conversely, absence of a sash does not prove she is not bedouin; some women living near agricultural villages have given up the sash as too traditional an item of dress for them to wear now. They appear to be in the minority, however.

The sashes come in heavy cottons, poplins, or sateens like the dresses but they differ with respect to their electric colors of red, fuchsia, and blue. Most beautiful are the ready-made woven wool sashes with fringed edges that frequently are tied with one corner pointing in a V down the back and the fringe protruding like a short grass skirt from the waist. These sashes that the Northern bedouin wear are made in Idqu on the coast near Rashid (Rosetta).

People in North Sinai report that the color of the sash makes a difference — that, for example, blue means a married woman, red an unmarried one, green a divorced woman. But even in the locality where these differences are mentioned, evidence suggests that these distinctions are not well maintained: almost every visible woman wears a red sash whether she is a *bint* (unmarried virgin) or not. Others claim that the sashes are a tribal marker but if this is true then the distinction is at the broadest level of generality, for red sashes are by far the most popular of the whole northern coast, both in Sinai and further west.

It is not unusual to find a discrepancy like this between what people say exists and what is observed to exist. Either such customs existed with more regularity in the recent past or the principle still stands for anyone to use as they see fit. Peoples of the Middle East are not so rigidly legalistic about rules as people in the West. If young unmarried girls are expected to be less adorned than married women, it is the intention that counts, as well as the local definition of whether adornment means bright colors, heavy embroidery, extensive jewelry, or a certain kind of dress. All things are relative. When people state an invariable rule they are usually only giving evidence of what they regard as important categories. In this case, the rules about sashes may indicate no more than that tribal distinctions and marital statuses are still significant categories for bedouin.

There are similar discrepancies with regard to what people say about the *burqa* (face veil). People reported that an unmarried woman wears a burqa of plain red material without coin or embroidered decorations. In North Sinai, unmarried women we observed wore no face veils until they married. After they don a modesty shawl at about age ten they are careful to cover their noses and mouths with a corner of the heavy shawl when in the presence of strangers.[3]

People also said that divorced women take off the burqa and revert again to pulling the modesty garment over the lower half of the face like unmarried girls but I had no chance to substantiate that information.

3. Saudi bedouin women wear black mask-like veils after puberty that cover their entire faces with the exception of slits for the eyes. The time of puberty for all bedouin groups is a time for more circumspect and modest behavior for young girls.

Married women of North Sinai display their wealth by making their face veils as elaborate as possible. Rows of metal coins extend vertically down the center "nose" line and culminate in medallion-like clumps of coins at the center front hem of the veil. Sometimes women add cloth streamers with coins at either side of the face, hanging behind the veil and sometimes circling the forehead. Coins may virtually cover the whole veil but more often they outline the bottom edge. The quantity of coins and whether they are gold or silver indicates the prosperity of the wearer. The arrangement of coins often mimics the line of at least one hidden feature, most often the nose but sometimes the eyebrows, the mouth or the ears.[4] Other pieces of jewelry may hang around the woman's neck or more coins may be sewn to strips of cloth to hang below the level of the face veil.

The cloth foundation of the face veil is light-weight and varies in color of material. Red is the most common color but yellow is also sometimes found along the north coast of Sinai. The bedouin veil differs from the half veil that one occasionally sees in the oasis (which hangs under the nose and only covers the mouth). The bedouin veil hangs from a narrow strand attached to a woven headband that circles the head at the forehead. Spreading gradually from this point, it covers the nose, mouth, and neck areas completely and extends to the chest or in some cases as far as the waist. The eyes, part of the forehead, and all of the cheeks remain visible. More properly this kind of veil is called a *litham* to differentiate it from the more masklike covering of the Arabian Peninsula. The Sinai veil is easily lifted over the head and left under the tarha to leave the face completely free when no one of consequence is around. Many bedouin women, however, remain veiled all the time, even, I am told, when they sleep.

For normal everyday wear, young unmarried girls (from about the age of ten), and adult women cover themselves with a black, undecorated, heavy, coarse shawl called a *gina'*. For better occasions and accompanied with their heavily embroidered dresses they wear a medium-weight, beautifully draping modesty cover that is extensively embroidered to match the embroidery of the dress. This large cover is designed so that when a piece about a third of the length is folded back and this double-layered part is laid over the head, the design matches over the whole length of the back and extends to just the point where the embroidery of the back panel of the dress takes over. Seen from the front of the wearer almost no embroidery except that in a band along the hem and sides of the dress is visible, while from the back, the entire human figure is draped with the exquisite embroidery. People explain that to decorate the front would be to attract the attention of men to the face of the wearer which would be immodest. But

---

4. This is most obvious in some Saudi face masks which replace the nose with lines of pearls, the eyebrows with small, loose, brass pointed pieces, the eyebrows with a line of silver woven threads, the cheeks with a line of coins, and the mouth with a similar line. The edges of the short mask are held down with large silver balls that dangle as if from ears.

Poor bedouin near Arish in
everyday dress.

to attract their attention to the back of the woman (and incidently to the sewing
skills that prove the suitability of the woman for marriage) after she has passed
is not of so immodest a character. This back view must be one of the most beautiful seen anywhere in costume history, since even though the human form is
successfully hidden, the gracefully flowing garments, and the lovely muted colors
give the impression that something of great substance and mystery has passed.

This modesty garment and others like it of similar size set boundaries to
the areas where it is practical to embroider basic dress garments underneath. Though
the modesty garment may be quite enveloping, its slipperiness and need for continuous arrangement means that side panels of dresses, sleeves, and occasionally

North Sinai bedouin dress
and modesty outfit with
face veil.

bodice bibs come into view from time to time. By working these areas, the wearer
can deceive the viewer into believing that the whole underdress is covered by
elaborate embroidery. The area which is least likely to be seen at the shoulders
and neck is often patched with spare pieces of bright material. On the North
Sinai dresses this still leaves large patches of dress embroidered. By contrast, the
South Sinai dress is much less heavily embroidered with work primarily concentrated on bib and sleeves.

The bedouin dress may be a marvel of patchwork black pieces particularly
if it is old and frequently repaired. Bedouin women are not notoriously neat
seamstresses in the construction of the basic dress, but at least until recently their
embroideries have been exquisitely detailed and neat, with subtle shadings of
vegetable dyes in soft reds, yellows, oranges, blues, and greens that blend into

an overall pleasing shading of color. Recent embroideries have stronger synthetic colors, use larger cross stitches, and generally are characterized by a greater carelessness in design and workmanship. Recent innovations include the addition of sequins, small reflecting mirrors, applique pieces, and sometimes machine-stitched flowers over part of the garment.

There is little interest in keeping up the quality of earlier designs and stitching. Bedouin girls who go to school, like peasant girls, wear either uniforms or clothes of a modern foreign style considered more appropriate to the educated. School girls do not have the years required to execute fine embroideries and in any case they invest their time in education as a more successful way of attracting potential mates. Their interest in more "sophisticated" styles has its impact on other non-school-goers who, even if they do not reject tribal outfits altogether, are not as willing to invest so much time in their construction. Contemporary tribal dresses reflect this carelessness. Since, however, few bedouin girls go beyond the early years of school there is little immediate danger of them leaving the tribal environment as some of their educated brothers do.

Women embroider on pieces of garment they carry around before final construction. An evenly woven material is attached to the black dress material to act as a guide for the cross stitch work and then is removed when the pattern is finished. The pattern is achieved by counting the stitches of the model being copied. Women do not create their own patterns; rather they copy those patterns of the mothers or relatives who instruct them. As a result there is a fairly long-term stability to patterns of local tribal segments or family groupings. It seems to be more a question of local imitation (or lack of creative initiative) that has caused patterns to become associated with certain tribal groupings, rather than a conscious attempt to distinguish one group from another. When the worked pieces are combined, seams are embroidered over to bring the patterns of two different sections together. Embroidered pieces often last longer than the background material. Women cut out the worked pieces and transfer them from dress to dress as the background material wears through, or they simply patch the background.

Described below are embroidery patterns said to be associated with particular tribal groupings in specific localities of Northern Sinai. Examples were brought in by women of these tribes and identified as being characteristic of the patterns found in areas where they were settled. My own observation of the areas however, revealed a great deal of variety and little consistency in embroidery patterns in these towns of the Northern Sinai.

> 1. *Rowda* — Pattern 1: There is a small stylized flower bud stem and two leaves on the diagonal forming a square. Squares are assembled to form either geometrically shaped panels or long vertical outlines. Pattern 2: Another form closer to nature appears as a vine of leaves with alternating colors. Closer in-

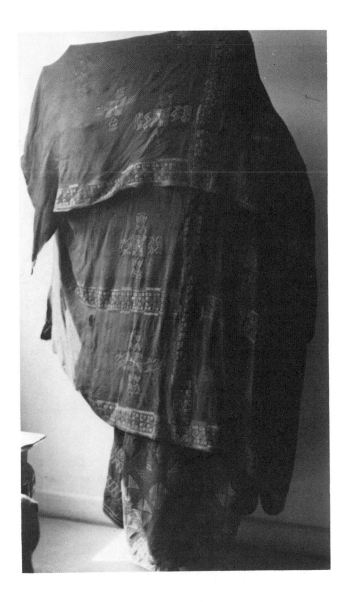

North Sinai bedouin
dress and modesty outfit.

spection shows the vine as a series of circles and Vs and the leaves abstractly
squared. Rowda patterns over all appear petite, tight, and regularly replicated.
They are usually executed in red.

2. *Bir al Abd:* The opposite extreme of the petite geometric Rowda pattern
is the large overall design of Bir al Abd which again represents a flower and
its leaves. This time the leaves circle in extravagant curves joined by a stem
and fixed to a small rectangular base. Instead of being joined by a vine, flow-

North Sinai woman
in everyday dress
displays her best dress with
hand-embroidered detail.

ers are placed side by side like individual plants. The flower blossom appears as a cross section. This design comes mainly in red. At a distance this pattern, elaborated and enlarged, looks like a series of square worked patches. It is usually found in reds.

3. *Abu Hamra:* This pattern fits somewhere between the two extremes above. The flower is more natural than the geometric Rowda pattern but the design parallels it in the use of geometric details to represent a vine connecting the flowers around a border. Overall the design appears more feathery than the stolid Bir al Abd flower patches. The patterns are most often found in blue.

4. *Arish:* In and around Arish the patterns begin to resemble the patterns of Palestine more closely. Palestinian patterns tend to be more complicated and varied, sometimes more real-to-life (as in a pattern with realistic vines and bunches of grapes) and sometimes abstracting patterns in geometric ways unrelated to natural models. Common to these patterns are S-shapes, arrows, triangles, and branching stylized designs of the tree-of-life. Even when flowers are the models, Palestinian patterns often abstract nature in fanciful and

Older woman's more elaborate
dress (front view).

usually delicately molded designs. Next to the sophistication of Palestinian
patterns, Sinai patterns are country cousins, awkward, heavy, stolid, and rarely
graceful, delicate or fanciful.

In patterns of dresses near Arish however, one begins to find a greater
delicacy in certain details of the design — a gently curving flower petal, more
detail in the flower parts, and a sense of feathery rather than totally solid
designs. The Sinai, as one would expect, provides a transition in styles from
the bedouin of Egypt to those of the Asian continent.

The patterns above were identified by bedouin as coming from specific localities. Another way they refer to them is to note a specific tribal grouping which
wears a particular pattern or a favored color. For example, the Abidiyah often

North Sinai dress with older sleeve type (Bir al Abd).

use a particular design executed in blue thread and they live mostly in the Sinai village of Abu Hamra. The Kharsa who live in Romana, Rowda, and Bir al Abd use red for their designs. Other groups who frequent the towns also have distinctive patterns that they hand down among their female relatives. As a result dresses in towns may be uniform or not depending on who happens to be present in the locality at any one time. This makes it difficult for a casual observer to find consistency in the patterns of an area.

The confusion of patterns in the towns of North Sinai should not by now be surprising. In many respects it parallels the experience of agricultural towns that cater to a hinterland. The town brings together, either temporarily or permanently, representatives of a number of surrounding influences, not to speak of the urban "sophisticate" government employees imposed on the area, and long-distance travellers passing through. Dress is still sufficiently varied to distinguish major categories of "us" and "them," to convey many personalized meanings and social statuses even if some of the more specific tribal distinctions have become somewhat blurred. A local embroidery pattern is not, after all, a necessary ingredient in the face-to-face recognition of one's friends and any non-local design is still sufficiently different to distinguish a stranger at a glance. Friend and stranger may now be the significant categories in any town big enough to bring the two together.

The example of one tribe semi-settled in the Arish area illustrates a present-day lack of dogmatism in dress designs as well as some of the influences affecting bedouin dress at present. The Sawarka is an outcast tribe from the days, it is reported, when a woman of the tribe was asked to take a message to the Prophet Muhammed and instead gave it to his enemies. They live in the area west of Arish toward Rafa; some have begun to farm land in areas the government is trying to reclaim after the Sinai was returned to Egypt.

In a tent reinforced with wood siding near the airport of Arish lives one of these farming Sawarka families, a sheikh, his two wives, and eight children. The dresses of the wives of the sheikh were of fine quality, with detailed heavy embroidery in the traditional style. The embroidery covered lower front and back and side panels with a heavily embroidered square at the neck and along the top of the sleeve arm. Most of the embroidery was red with a few details in blue, yellow, and orange. The women wore, for everyday, unembroidered black dresses, heavy black tarhas, red sashes, and heavily encrusted face masks with gold coins. In other words, there was little that was distinctive about the dress from a traditional perspective.

Another family of Sawarka, a few miles distant from the first, and poorer, lived in huts made of brush and poles and reinforced with tent pieces. The one wife, her two daughters, and daughter-in-law wore dresses that incorporated a number of modern elements into the design. Heavy embroidery was concentrated in a rectangular bib front and along the top of the sleeve from shoulder to wrist. The design which was similar to that of the other Sawarka family was composed of a series of large rosettes, divided by embroidered lines to emphasize their formation in rows. Like the first family, also, the bodice designs were executed mainly in red but with yellows, oranges, and blues added for accent. The second family also wore red sashes and heavy black undecorated tarhas. Where their dress differed from the more traditional family was in the skirt design which consisted of machine-embroidered flowers, leaves, and stems over the whole area of the skirt from the thigh to floor. Each flower center contained a small circular mirror that glittered as the woman walked. This work was done by men who by profession do this kind of machine decorating on bed sheets, night gowns, and other clothing that townspeople buy. The machine work was all in blue, contrasting with the mostly red work of the bib embroidery. The women remarked that the machine work looked more beautiful. It certainly saved them considerable time, though at the cost of paying the men for the work.

Affluent bedouin family of two wives and children in everyday attire. Young
girl wears plain modesty cover. Face veils display family wealth.

The young women of this same family had a second set of clothes that they
used for visiting Arish. The dress, one that normally distinguishes townspeople
from bedouin in that town, is described below. Its use by the bedouin demonstrates the current strong attraction of urban styles and the willingness of at least
a few of this particular tribe to obscure their bedouin origins in the context of
the town. Given the unusual position of the Sawarka as "outcast" bedouin working in the disdained (for a bedouin) occupation of farming, it is perhaps not surprising to find some of them willing to adopt an urban dress with more status
in the modern world. Their stake in the bedouin hierarchy of status is low; if
they can pass in the anonymous town at a higher level, simply by donning suitable clothing, they have little to lose.

The urban dress of Arish and the fishing villages near Arish is unique in
Egypt but not, according to people from Arish, in other parts of the Middle East.
They say that it is the same as the dress worn traditionally by Palestinians. Most
people agree that it was not so commonly worn in Arish before 1967 but after

Bedouin woman of North Sinai: upper dress bodice handworked, skirt section machine-stitched with small mirrors in contemporary fashion.

the disastrous 1967 defeat of Egypt at the hands of the Israelis and the occupation of the Sinai, the dress became more common. Some say this happened because people became more religious in the wake of the defeat (and their apparent abandonment by God), causing women to revert to dress that covered their bodies and heads more decorously. Others say the dress was a statement by the people in Arish of their Arab and Palestinian sympathies under Israeli occupation.

The urban dress of Arish, commonly seen alongside "foreign" dress, consists of a long black gathered skirt reaching to mid-calf or ankle length, a colored, usually print, blouse, and a white lightweight tarha.[5] The skirt, called a *da'ira* (meaning a circle of cloth),[6] is made of a medium-weight material. The blouse can be of any print or plain color. Its top is obscured by the large tarha which is wrapped around the head and drapes over the shoulders. One corner covers the mouth and is tucked into the side of the scarf near the ear. Sometimes the tarha is embroidered with small flowers. The whole costume is very different from any other in Egypt.

BEDOUIN OF SOUTHERN SINAI

The major division of bedouin in Sinai follows a north and south split. Bedouin concentrate in the more moderate regions in the north near the coast and in the south in the hills that lead up to the monastery of St. Catherine. In both areas, underground water makes it possible for some date farming to go on as well as the watering of flocks. Both areas are crisscrossed by routes that at one time were significant in camel caravan trade. Now bedouin own trucks with which they provide the same kinds of services for towns along the routes.

People of the Sinai recognize distinctive dress differences between bedouins of north, south, inland, and coastal areas. The most important however, occur between south and north, which to all intents and purposes overlap the inland and coastal differences. Even men's dress which does not serve as often as a distinctive marker of locality differs between the two areas. Northern bedouin men, for example, wear a navy-colored abaya cloak while southern men wear a brown cloak like the Saudis.[7] Women's dress as usual is more elaborated and conveys a much more distinctive appearance.

The South Sinai women modify the basic foundation black bedouin dress with a *kornish* (hem ruffle) that is outlined in subtle colors with embroidery where it joins the main part of the skirt. Otherwise the black skirt and the lower bodice is

5. In Palestine this white head covering has several names. Among the ones I have heard are *shumbar, yanus,* and *negab.* Peasant women are said to wear white scarves and bedouin black ones.
6. The skirt is also sometimes called *tanoura* in Levantine Arabic. Egyptians usually mean an underslip by the term. Da'ira (skirt or literally, circle of cloth) elsewhere in Egypt was used to identify the skirt part of the now extinct two-piece hubbara (see Chapter 8).
7. It is interesting that the South Sinai woman's dress also shares similarities with dress of the Saudi Nejd. There women wear cotton thawbs that are ankle length with narrow sleeves embroidered in geometric lines and edged with silver bells at the wrist. The rest of the dress is plain (Ross 1980).

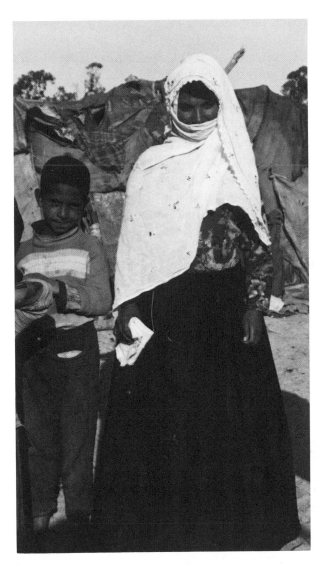

Bedouin woman of North Sinai, dressed for a visit into the town of Arish,
wearing typical urban dress for that town.

undecorated. In this dress the decorative work is concentrated on the heavily
worked narrow sleeves, a front upper bodice and sometimes the sash. The sleeves
are embroidered over almost their entire area. Colored thread is used also for
the front bodice bib except in the case of rich women who can afford to substitute beading for thread. The sash may be all red with no decoration, but in

wealthier dress it may be white with tiny diamond-shaped beading in reds, yellows, and blues.

The face mask for ordinary home use is three-tiered with edging at each layer of material. An outside mask covers all the features of the face except the eyes and is decorated with long rows of coins in a central stripe, and with rows of coins along the bottom edge. Unmarried girls are said to wear undecorated material of any color to cover their faces.

Over the outfit a woman wears an *aba'*, a heavy woven garment in black with woven stripes in green, light yellow, and red around the edge, and perpendicular to the edge at the crown and at the sides of the head. In general the dress of these mountain dwellers tends to be cut somewhat narrower along the arms and body to preserve body heat during the cold seasons.

The dress of the South Sinai bedouin is immediately recognizable as very different from that described above for North Sinai bedouin, and shows even greater contrast with the bedouin of the north coast of Egypt proper.

North Coast of Egypt Distinctions

The bedouins of the north coast of Egypt proper adjusted some time ago to a more sedentary way of life. Their bedouin origins reveal themselves, however, in the frequent use of tents erected next to substantial low-lying cement houses for the shelter of their animals. Bedouin of the northern coast tend also to place their homes at a distance from their neighbors that would correspond to the spatial arrangements of their tents were they still following a nomadic existence. Desert-style, the windows of their homes are small and the house resembles the low outline of a tent. These bedouin have several sources of income: sheep herding, fig farming, and renting their tribal lands to Egyptian urbanites to build vacation homes along the shore. As if to symbolize their long-term adjustment to sedentary life the dress of the northern bedouin is least "bedouin-like," and more closely resembles peasant dress.

Northern Coast bedouin dresses are bright-colored, flowered or black, ankle-length, with long narrow sleeves. They are usually waisted and many still are belted with the bedouin-style bright-colored scarf wrapped around the waist, frequently with a fringed corner hanging down the center of the back. The head is covered with a head scarf and sometimes a tarha is added over that, tied in the bedouin fashion behind the head at ear level. Sometimes these women add a colored band over the headgear and across the forehead to hold the headgear in place. They do not wear any more engulfing modesty garment.

Despite the resemblance of these basic dresses to peasant dress, the sashes and manner of tying the head scarf still confirm the wearer's bedouin origin. In coastal towns like Hammam and Burg al-Arab, peasants are still easily distinguishable from bedouin by their "sophisticate" folk styles or by the folk style known to be characteristic of Alexandria (but hardly ever seen in the city itself any more).

Alexandria Style

The Alexandria dress is one of the most beautiful of the folk peasant dresses, reminiscent of early nineteenth-century "shepherdess" styles in Europe. It has leg-of-mutton (full high-standing) sleeves, narrowing to cuffed wrists. The bodice is shirred horizontally with a central stitching line and tight fitting below the bust to the waist. The skirt is mid-calf to ankle length. The most elegant of these dresses come in black or other dark-colored velvet. A tarha completes the outfit.

The Alexandria dress is found now primarily in two areas. The first is in the countryside north and northwest of Damenhour along the Mahmoudiyya and Idku canals and along the Rashid (or Rosetta) branch of the Nile. There the incidence of the waisted Alexandria dress in urban areas coincides with the presence of *careta,* colorful horse-drawn carts that are so prominent a feature of coastal towns like Abu Kir. The appearance of these coastal influences are abruptly felt from the time one leaves the northwestern fringes of Damenhour, revealing again the significance of waterways in penetrating and exerting substantial influence on hinterlands (see also Fayoum).[8] The second area where the Alexandria dress is found is in the small coastal towns like Burg al Hammam where peasant-bedouin distinctions are still of some importance but there, as in the areas mentioned above, urban sophisticate styles (see Chapter 6) have often diluted the strength of its incidence.

Another important group of the coast distinguishable through dress is that of the salt-water and inland coastal fishermen. They are most easily recognized in the dress of the men.

Fisherfolk of the Northern Coast

The most distinctive element in the fishermen's dress are the black pants (*sirwall*) which are extremely baggy in the crotch and fairly tight-fitting along calf and at the ankle. They are identical with the *shirwaal* pants of peasants in Lebanon and Syria. The outfit is completed with a tight-fitting knit shirt or a loose cotton blouse, sidari vest, a cummerbund at the waist and, in cold weather, some kind of loose jacket. Sometimes a simple, button-front, modern shirt is all that covers the torso. A scarf wrapped tightly around the head composes the head covering.

---

8. The Alexandria dress however should not be confused with waisted moda styles like the *qasat cloche* and the *sha'af cloche* (see Chapter 6).

Everyday Alexandria dress
from near Mahmudiya in
Boheira governorate.

In Egypt this distinctive outfit is often associated exclusively with groups which engage in fishing, but it is also seen elsewhere among peasants in Kafr il Sheikh and Boheira. For example, between Idfina and Rashid (Rosetta), on the Rashid branch of the Nile, the majority of fruit and date grove workers still wear the outfit. The small museum in Rashid shows the close connection of the town with Turkish influences. In historical tableaux of the last century, townspeople appear in dress that very closely resembles the "fisherman's" outfit of today. All over the contemporary Middle East this Turkish influence remains in the incidence of baggy shirwaal pants, worn in Lebanon and Syria by farmers, and in Saudi Arabia as underwear under thawb shirt dresses. It is plausible that the pants have survived so long in Egypt among date farmers and fishermen because of

Everyday Alexandria dress
from a village in the
central Delta.

their intrinsic practicality in occupations that require a great deal of mobility.
The alternative, the galabiya, is much more restrictive a garment on boats and
in climbing date palms.[9]

RED SEA COAST INHABITANTS

In the third and final major desert area of Egypt, the Eastern or Arabian Desert,
there are three identifiable social groups: in the north, the Arab bedouin, related
to groups in the Sinai and wearing similar dress; in the middle regions, the
'Ababdah, (a Hamitic group); and on the Red Sea Coast to as far as the Sudan,

9. This does not prevent date growers inland and Nile boatmen from wearing galabiyas, however.

the Beja (which include the Bishariin and other tribal segments also related to Hamitic groups. The Beja have their own language, speaking Arabic only as a second language. The tribal segments engage variously in fishing, trading (dried fish, coffee, drugs, camels, charcoal, and household staples), and animal husbandry (camel, goats, and sheep) and often observe prohibitions against intermarriage with other lineages.

Beja

The Beja wear a distinctive dress[10] which like that of the Mediterranean fishermen takes its inspiration from foreign origins, this time from India by way of Port Sudan and camel caravan to Egypt. The women dress in bright-colored, yellow and red saris of expensive materials if they are wealthy, and light-weight gauze cottons if they are poorer. The well-to-do also wear nose rings. Wealthy men wear baggy white shirwaal-type pants of fine material and a long blue tunic-like vest. Poorer Beja wear less fine materials or alternatively, a tunic-like short galabiya top over pants.

Despite their extensive travels, trading fish to Qena and camels to Daraw among other contacts, the Beja remain, as far as Egypt is concerned, a backwater of unique dress styles. In truth, however, it is their extensive travels to the distant markets of the Sudan that has provided them with dress models unavailable to more sedentary Egyptians.

Generally speaking, Egyptian culture does not actively encourage its members to seek individual rewards in life, nor does it provide many fields where people can seek recognition for their individual accomplishments. Individuals receive their strength from social groups and their recognition from how well they support these groups. Dress recognizes this fact. Distinctive patterns reflect allegiances to ethnic community, regional locality, and units of special ecological adaptation. Each, until recently, has been assured of the moral superiority of his or her way of life. At the same time, dress is also a product of pragmatic forces, affected by a particular physical environment, the accidents of place and time, and the invasion of foreign influences that have come to be invested with local significance. The complex of factors affecting the final outcomes in dress is not easily nor even advisably separated into component parts, or assigned impact weightings in too categorical a way. It is best to see dress as a fluid medium of diverse and complex origins.

10. *Beja* dress descriptions were kindly related to me by Diana DeTreuville who has studied groups along the Red Sea Coast.

Presentation of Self

"Under the veils there is lethal poison"
"Dress up a piece of reed and it will become a bride"
"Even if she puts on burlap, she is still Aisha"
"If the personality itself does not impress, the clothes will not impress"
"While the mother of Isa dresses, church will let out"
"He fills his clothes"—Arab proverbs

WHILE GROUP NORMS typically dictate fairly close adherence to customary forms of dress, there is still usually room for individuals to choose between a range of styles or between elements in a particular style. To do so within certain limits is usually not to transgress the bounds of propriety.

Individual choice in dress depends on a balance of factors: circumstances (*zuruf*)—what is available and what the person can afford; the common understandings of society about dress—including such set repertoires as those of place and community described above; and finally, individual desires about how the person wants to present the self to the world. The first two set limits on choice that an individual can do little about. The third requires judgments and decisions. There is enough variation in outcome to keep the combination of dress elements a fluid and changing phenomenon. For the individual, each set of factors is like a celluloid overlay that contributes greater nuance and detail to the final product.

General social and cultural understandings about dress serve as a generating grammar in the language of dress while the varied expressions represent mere surface manifestations, constrained by the rules of the grammar but not determined solely by its outlines. A young woman, for example, may wear all the proper modesty garb so that technically in the community she is beyond reproach. But in the manner of holding her cloak, in the amount of ankle she exposes, in the way the dress fits, she can present to appropriate audiences as alluring and provocative a demeanor as though she were baring her naked flesh. One interpretation of the proverb, "The clever woman can spin even with the leg of a donkey" expresses the possibilities extant in the most limiting of instruments.

Social communities wrestle with the dialectic of opposing goals and finally dictate to their members by their norms and values where the thresholds of moderation and approved behavior lie. Khuri notes this when he comments, "[There is] no single yardstick, cultural or otherwise by which modesty, honor and shame may be measured. These vary with economic classes. A mini-skirt worn by an affluent is fashion, by a self-sufficient, it is presumption, by a poor person, it indicates immodesty" (Khuri 1975:87, 88).

People without a strong sense of personal assertiveness automatically accept the identities of their social group, especially when they live in homogeneous communities unchallenged by conflicting ideas or styles. Others feel the tension between wanting to conform with group norms and a desire to express personal uniqueness. Dress is at the same time a way of showing membership in the group —as when all women of a household wear dresses from the same bolt of material or children wear the uniforms of their school—and a way of asserting one's differences from the group—by a greater attractiveness, higher economic or social status, etc. For the individual, dress is also a marker of the commonplace and a marker of special events and special places. This chapter examines some of the choices an Egyptian faces in the presentation of self and some of the common Egyptian social understandings associated with markers of personal identities.

The markers of place and community discussed in earlier chapters usually reflect understandings that have been in existence a long time. Most people select their basic styles from within the conventional range that includes many of these markers. If they want to convey an individualized meaning about self, they turn either to a manipulation of the elements in conventional dress or they adopt a pattern that has come to have invested in it a higher value in the society. Today, it is often patterns generated in urban areas that hold the most attraction for individuals trying to break out of the narrow confines of local tastes. Assuming such innovations, however, can pose a risk for an individual if neighbors feel that local ways are being rejected or attacked.

URBAN IDENTIFIERS

In stressing the dress patterns which are markers of place and community, we have neglected the folkstyles which are probably the most common in contemporary Egypt—the "urban sophisticate" styles. They are so labelled to indicate that they identify the dress of a large number of urban dwellers and the few rural people who want to demonstrate a more sophisticated knowledge of urban life styles. The styles include overdress modesty garments, cloak-style wraps, and modifications of everyday women's and men's galabiyas.

One woman's wardrobe (peasant, Delta).

Women's Folk Sophisticate Styles

Moda Overdress (style one)

The most common of the sophisticate styles is the moda overdress described here. Ubiquitous among the Cairene lower class, it has come to have associations with that largest city in Egypt. The overdress is fully gathered like the yoked granny style basic dress found commonly in prints or solid colors in the Delta.

Urban family of three generations wearing folk dress: three women in
moda styles, and one in front row in fitted style; foreign styles on three
males and one girl in slacks; and fundamentalist style on girl in back row.

The difference is that as a modesty garment it always appears in solid black material of shiny satin, jersey, silk, or heavy cotton. A narrow edging of black lace
outlines the yoke and sometimes the collar if there is one. The sleeves are full
to accommodate other layers of clothing underneath.

The overdress conceals the basic dress which may be waisted, fitted or a
granny style like the overdress. It is most popular among busy married women
because of its practicality. The dress can be thrown on to dash out on an errand
and, because it is constructed as a dress, it does not need to be continually fussed
with to keep it covering the essential parts of the woman. This style is said by
many to have originated among the lower classes of Cairo where it became common only in the last fifteen years.

Increasing numbers of women now don the overdress as a "uniform" to wear
in public from about the age of fourteen. It is also now found commonly in large
parts of the Delta and, infrequently, in cities of Upper Egypt. The style represents

Melas.

all that is undesirable to those who would retain the variety and beauty of traditional costumes, since it is usually crudely constructed with little decorative addition that is distinctive. Women sometimes call it "moda," which means that it is currently fashionable. The style is now becoming so commonplace that in some areas this appellation is no longer appropriate.

Overdress (style two)

A more localized sophisticate style, confined to certain cities of the Delta, has little incidence elsewhere. Called a *melas* (the name refers to the material that is used to make it up), this black overdress is a commodious garment in general outline like the squared-off jubba of Upper Egypt with the same deep placket neckline but small hand slits left open on the sides rather than at the top edge.

The distinctive feature of the melas is its puckered textile that drapes in regular parallel lines of gathers every eight inches or so, in the style of Viennese draped curtains. Since the melas does not cover the head, it is commonly topped with a scarf, tarha, or shawl. The melas is occasionally seen in many towns of the Delta, but its main incidence as an overdress is seen in the towns and occasionally the villages of Sharqiya, especially in rural towns like Abu Kabir. Sharqiya's traditional ties with Upper Egypt tend to encourage a more conservative approach to dress, particularly in urban areas where strangers abound. The melas is definitely a style associated with urban life though now it is not unusual to see village women donning the garment on formal occasions or for visits to the city.

Overdress (style three)

Another localized urban style seen particularly in Abu Kabir in Sharqiya but sometimes also elsewhere in the Delta is the *bedla* (literally "suit") dress. Its full-length wide A-line[1] style from shoulder to floor with sleeves that widen at the wrist make it very similar to the usual folk style galabiya men wear. The woman's dress, however, is usually made up in a heavy black cloth like "smoking," a heavy corded rayon material that is more expensive than most of the materials used for folk styles. Again it may be topped by any of the three basic head coverings, but is usually worn with a black scarf or tarha.

Wrap (style one)

Very common in the large cities of Egypt, particularly Cairo, the *melaya liff* is a special favorite of young women who make use of its seductive potential.

1. A-line in Arabic is called iid w rigil, literally hand and foot, which refers to the way it is cut on the bias, matching a corner from the top of the material across to the bottom opposite corner.

To wear this wrap is to be continually occupied with its slippery and voluminous folds. This modesty cloak (*melaya* is a general term for covering and *liff* refers to the way it is wrapped around the body) predates the moda overdress (style one). The melaya is a slinky large rectangle of shiny nylon, silk, or other thin, clinging material. The black opaque cloth ostensibly conceals the figure but because it is light and clingy may reveal more than it conceals of the shape underneath.

A woman wears the melaya liff over her head or draped across her shoulders and flowing to her ankles. It is in this way of carrying and adjusting the melaya that it can become a provocative form-revealing item of apparel. Commonly when walking, a woman gathers up the bottom half, pulls it tightly around her and lets the ends hang over one arm; in back view, the shape and movement of her buttocks are clearly visible under the cloak. The "entrapping" quality of the melaya is expressed in the proverb, "She spread out her melaya for him," which means she scolded him. The melaya liff, associated originally with the city, has spread rapidly through the Delta and among the more worldly of the Upper Egyptians. Egyptian Christians tend to associate the melaya liff with Muslim use but that distinction is not strictly observed in contemporary Egypt.

Wrap (style two)

Rarely seen, this wrap has the quality of the melaya liff in that it occupies its wearer with continuous readjustment. In material and cut it combines the melas overdress and the melaya liff. Also called a melas because of its gathered, draped rows of cloth, this garment consists of a length of cloth wrapped around the wearer in the style of the melaya liff. It is thus differentiated from the melas of Sharqiya that is constructed in the shape of a commodious but still definable dress donned over the head. This melas wrap style is found predominantly in the capital of Boheira province, Damenhour, again primarily as an urban phenomenon but also often seen on villagers visiting the city or on other formal occasions.

Basic Dresses

Other urban sophisticate styles include modifications of basic dresses. These styles which often start among the lower classes in towns and are inexpensive soon spread to rural areas with such rapidity that the length of time they are considered urban and sophisticated is limited. These dresses include the *galabiya rigali,* a fitted dress (see under Male-Female identities in Chapter 6), and the cloche (see under Youth-Maturity in Chapter 6). In many ways they are more appropriately labelled fashionable at the moment.

Women's urban sophisticate styles worn in the village are a sign of a folk person's acquaintance with urban ways—thus the use of the term "sophisticate"

Bedla (left) and *melas* (right) near Abu Kebir.

here. Eventually, however, a sophisticate style may become so widespread in an urban or even in a rural area that it loses its potency as a status symbol. In many areas of Egypt, especially in the Delta, this has become true for the granny moda overdress and the melaya liff described above. In these areas, the styles have become convention. The style then no longer holds the special personalized meanings that attract attention in the way that less common styles do. Fakhouri, studying a large village near Cairo, notes that the only public dress appropriate for long-established women residents of the village is a black cotton or silk galabiya which he says is a symbol of maturity and stability (Fakhouri 1972:21).

Worn in the city, sophisticate styles erase identifying markers of country origins, permitting the woman to blend in to the anonymity of urban society. The concept of sophistication is therefore relative with regard to dress. Some sophisticate styles described above are so regional in their identification with city life that they are seen as provincial by big-city Cairenes, and similarly, styles that are commonplace in the city may seem sophisticated in the rural context. The rural

Melaya liff.

woman will often don sophisticate styles to go shopping in the city. This way she marks her knowledge of what is correct without incurring the risk that her action might be construed as presumption by other villagers. In the city she may want to obscure her origins to appear less conspicuous. She may also think that she looks less gullible as a customer when she masquerades as one familiar with the city. Her neighbors would be sympathetic to this pose, but they would be less sympathetic if they thought she donned these styles in order to behave in the morally doubtful way that they presume is the urban standard.

Though modesty styles are used to signal a woman's intent to behave properly, they do not guarantee that the observer will automatically accept the message being conveyed. With use of sophisticate styles the risk of misinterpretation rises inversely in relation to the level of acceptance in a particular area of the style. The first who wear such styles run greater risks whereas those who don the styles after they are commonplace run little risk. Eventually the style becomes, as Fakhouri notes, a symbol of maturity and stability. Those who wear more acceptably concealing overdresses, of course, run less risk than those who wear the slippery sophisticate wraps. Those who establish their credentials as "nice girls" by their demeanor, their education (which is supposed to make a girl more rational and responsible in many cases), or their family's reputation also run less risk but conversely are held to unequivocally proper behavior.

Some sophisticate styles, like the moda overdress and the galabiya rigali, are adopted because they are considered fashionable in the lower classes. As such they are more readily adopted by younger rather than older women. A woman in the oasis of Bahriya, which is connected by direct road to Cairo, showed me her wardrobe, describing it and the styles of the women in the oasis as follows:

> Here, in the town of Bawiti, only the old women wear the traditional dress of Bahriya. When my grandmother died a year ago, we put her embroidered dress on the top of the wardrobe and it has remained there ever since. We think it is old-fashioned. All the married women wear the galabiya bi suffra (the yoked granny dress) like women in Cairo. Mine are all in flowers and prints. When we go out of the house we cover ourselves with a futa (heavy shawl) or melaya liff, satiny and not as heavy as that of our grandmothers, but still larger than the ones worn in Cairo. We are still conservative here. When I go to Cairo on the bus, I wear a dress that is fitted at the waist and sometimes on visits to people there I wear short foreign-style dresses. [She pointed out how much nicer the effect of the fitted dress was when compared with the loose granny dress.] People here in Bawiti know how to dress!

This oasis woman is very conscious of the importance of appropriate behavior in different public and not-so-public contexts. She has compromised in her modesty attire by finding a style that lies somewhere between the extremes of her grandmother's standard and those of the city. She also showed me in her wardrobe a transparent nightgown which she said she wore when her husband was home, and an opaque one for when he was away on business. Similarly she had embroidered bed sheets for his nights at home and plain ones for when he was away. She pointed out that if relatives or friends dropped by it would not look right for her to have a provocative nightgown and fancy sheets when her

Oasis woman with Cairo-inspired everyday dress.

husband was not present. Several other young women of the oasis talked about wearing clothes styles like those of Cairo and all said they preferred to buy their materials in that city. Most either know how to sew themselves or have a close relative that sews.

Most folk sophisticate styles for women relate to modesty in some way—as overdresses and as wraps. It is appropriate that the elaboration of modesty styles should occur in cities where there are more strangers and consequently a greater need for protection. Historically a number of modesty garments were introduced through urban areas from outside Egypt, usually from Turkey during the time of the Ottoman Empire. The melaya liff is most certainly one of these. From urban centers the styles spread subsequently to hinterland towns and villages, and eventually lost the valued connotations of urban sophistication. Some of the modesty coverings characteristic of Upper Egyptian towns are relics of such earlier sophisticate styles.

Men's Folk Sophisticate Styles

Men's folk dress has been little mentioned in these pages, because as noted earlier, when compared with women's dress, men's dress distinguishes a much

Man in rural style and son in sophisticate style.

more limited range of meanings. One of the main values displayed in men's dress is the appreciation of urban styles (and coincidentally standards of prosperity). Ordinary folk males wear one of two standard versions of the galabiya described in Chapter 2. The versions vary primarily in the width of hem at ankle and wrist (usually very wide in the countryside, less wide in the city) and in different types of neck opening (a wide oval with open U-shaped extension in the country or a buttoned placket extension in the city). Beyond a tendency to differentiate city from village and, through the quality of materials, levels of affluence, these two standard galabiyas indicate little else.

New variations of the galabiya, however, have come to be viewed as modern and sophisticated. Some have been introduced directly into villages by workers

Men's styles: *Frangi* sophisticate [right figure]; *Scandarani* sophisticate
[center figure]; Standard peasant, left figure.

returning from abroad, others by university students home for holidays and re-
verting from foreign to folk dress. Because the styles are more often adopted by
young men keeping up with the times, they are also one way of distinguishing
the generations.

It is not uncommon to see a farmer visiting a town wearing a traditional
rural galabiya and holding the hand of a small toddler who is wearing a "sophis-

Young men's styles: left to right, rural *galabiya,* sophisticate style with *scandarani* neckline, and sophisticate style with *frangi* neckline.

ticate" style, a symbol of the father's aspirations for his son to rise to something higher on the scale of social value than he himself. On him it would be presumption; on his child it is "cute."

The two main sophisticate styles are the *galabiya frangi,* and the *galabiya scandarani* (Alexandria style).[2] They are both typically loose but more form-fitting than either standard styles of galabiya. They incorporate details recognized as foreign such as breast pockets, collars, and cuffs. Both styles have buttoned placket front openings and high necklines. The sleeves are narrow and frequently cuffed. The two styles differ in that the frangi has a shirt collar and the scandarani has a mandarin collar.

Another "sophisticate" style for men is the two-piece pajama set, worn for lounging around the house, for short excursions out into the street and also incidentally for sleeping in. Again the garment incorporates the foreign elements of pockets and collars, as well as the general style of pants and jacket. This style in the city has become so common that it has lost the value as designator of sophistication it still holds in many villages.

Why are the special markers in men's folk dress, when compared with wom-

2. This style as a sophisticate dress is quite different from the traditional woman's dress described elsewhere as an Alexandria dress (see Chapter 5).

en's dress, so heavily focused in marking levels of sophistication? Several factors may be relevant. Travel is generally the prerogative of the folk male, whether it be to nearby towns, faraway cities, or to foreign countries. He often seeks work outside the village, in cities and regional towns, on the river Nile with its increased boat traffic after the advent of the High Dam, or in the army. Increasingly men travel to other countries of the Arab world for work in construction and other manual labor. The similarity between the Saudi thawb and Egyptian sophisticate styles of the galabiya is not a coincidence. Rather it represents wealth, foreignness, and elegance to the rural peasant.

Acquaintance with urban ways is associated with buying power if a person is from the village, or with good wages from manual labor if one is a lower-class resident of the city. If a person is educated, then the city represents the place where opportunities are available for him to find work and escape from the drudgeries of agricultural labor. Consequently for the male peasant the urban-rural distinction is a significant one, carrying with it connotations of economic and social success. By contrast, women's connection with home and residence perpetuates the significance of markers of place in her dress. She is an asset of her community and as such advertises her connections to locale. Her use of sophisticate styles must be carried out with caution. On the one hand, it supports the image of family prosperity, but on the other if she disguises the markers of place, she may be criticized for immodesty, and may offend people for her presumption. Much depends as noted earlier on the way people in her village view sophisticate styles and her right to wear them.

To summarize then, certain of the sophisticate styles for both men and women, although technically covering the body in the way that is considered appropriate for Muslims, are in fact more revealing of the form than earlier styles either because the cloth is lighter weight and clings, or because the style is more fitted. Because they are worn more often by the young they are associated with what is daring and new. The melaya liff, the galabiya rigali, the galabiya frangi and galabiya scandarani all possess one or more of these characteristics. At the folk level, when compared with more conventional styles, sophisticate styles form the contrast modern-traditional. From the perspective of the middle classes, however, all folk styles are still considered "traditional."

LEVEL OF EDUCATION AND CLASS

The polar contrasts of educated-uneducated represent significant categories on a scale of present-day Egyptian social values. As mentioned earlier Egyptian dress is characterized by two basic types—folk and foreign—and those who wear one or the other are characterized by specific styles of life, social classes, and educational status. Dress thus marks what is a clear and recognized dichotomy in the social status and style of life of contemporary Egyptians. Adopting the dress of the new status is one way of making abundantly clear that a person has made the change.

Educated Egyptians wearing foreign dress pursue urban occupations in offices and stores; they live in apartment blocks with running water and electricity, own television sets, use over-stuffed furniture, send their children to schools, and spend their leisure time with their families. Egyptians who wear "traditional" dress live in the poorer quarters of urban areas or in modest dwellings in rural villages. They work as manual laborers or farmers. Their homes often do not have running water or electricity, the rooms are multi-functional, the furniture straight-forward and simple, appliances are uncomplicated and primitive. Many would like to see their children finish schooling and become government employees but they also find value in training their children in manual occupations that will give them higher incomes than their fathers. The men spend their leisure time in coffee shops, while the women socialize as they do chores in the morning or with relatives and friends at home in the evening.

Extended education is the major but not exclusive boundary between those who wear folk and those who wear foreign dress. Since education is thought to make people more rational, the socially mobile are permitted modified styles vastly different from those that are the norm in the lower classes. When children remain long in school they become eligible for middle-class life styles and status. Their middle-class teachers provide strong role models and, from the start, school uniforms of pants for the boys and modified pant suits for the girls provide the chance for many children to become accustomed to foreign dress. One of the obstacles lower-class parents cite as preventing them from sending their children to school is the high cost[3] of providing the uniforms, shoes and socks, briefcases, and other items they feel are necessary to the educational process.

Educated middle-class foreign dress was introduced to local populations most significantly by occupation forces who considered the dress appropriate for clerical, military, and industrial work. Later the styles took on the status of white-collar work, and the dress appropriate for the elites. Readers are familiar with the elements that make up foreign international dress: for women, skirts, blouses, two-piece suits, knit dresses, stockings, high-heeled shoes, and purses, and for men, shirts, pants, suits, socks, and shoes. Not many readers however may have considered the elements that make foreign dress critically different from folk dress.

Foreign dress is more costly because there is no modesty cover to hide the

3. In 1983, typical costs for school necessities included shoes (£E 3 or 4), socks (20p), uniforms (£E 1.50 including 50p as the cost of making the garment), a book bag (£E 4 or 5), pens, erasers, and notebooks (£E 1). At that time the dollar equalled the pound on the free market.

underdress, thus requiring a large wardrobe of varied colors and matching pieces. Separate dresses are required to match the occasion—for office work, for house-work and shopping, for pregnancy, for parties, for weddings, for visits, and for mourning. Items of clothing need to be replaced more quickly because the ma-terial is often not as durable (stockings, for example), because fashion changes more rapidly, and because the closer fit of the clothes makes them less amenable to changes in the size of the wearer.

The details of foreign dress not found in most folk dress, like collars, pockets, cuffs, zippers, etc. are difficult to make and usually require the costly skills of the professional. The clothes may need the special care of dry cleaning. Because a woman's hair is uncovered, its appearance becomes a cause for concern, requir-ing either time-consuming efforts at home or trips to the beauty parlor. The greater expanses of neck, arm, and leg visible, not to mention the more form-fitting na-ture of foreign dress, means that adjustments in bodily movement have to be made to preserve a decorous appearance.

One village widow about to be married to a widower who was a clerk in an urban government store demanded, as part of her bridal payment, the cost of the clothing she would need to purchase for her new status[4] as the wife of a middle-class government employee. The items of clothing she listed were those she thought vital to changing from folk to foreign dress: stockings, shorter dresses, high-heeled shoes, and a purse.

Dressing "foreign" is a critical marker of having achieved middle-class sta-tus. Were such strong connotations of positive value not associated with foreign dress, there would be little compensation for the major inconveniences foreign dress causes its wearers in Egypt. Besides being more economically costly, its styles and materials are environmentally unsuitable in many cases. The styles are con-stricting in comparison with folk styles: there is no fullness to allow for air cir-culation and the materials out of which most foreign dress is constructed are usu-ally synthetic nylons and knits. Perhaps in recognition of these disadvantages, a style similar to the two-piece safari outfits of British colonialist environments has become popular with men. This style does away with the need to wear shirts and ties and is made in short-sleeve cotton versions for the summer.

The strong social value associated with foreign dress can be best illustrated by the example of the Egyptian University dean who refused the request of fun-damentalist students to wear folk galabiyas on campus. He explained that gala-biyas were not appropriate dress for the educational environment.

Foreign dress is believed to reflect the greater sophistication of its wearer, who has had his mind opened by education. In this process he has become more

4. The widower, of peasant origin himself, was willing to marry a woman of a lower class because he had several children who had to be taken care of and thus was not interested in an educated woman who might have a more independent personality.

Urban children: girl in
foreign dress and boy in
folk dress.

widely acquainted with things foreign: languages, customs, and material objects. The educated commonly use foreign words and phrases like "merci," "tante," and "pardon," prefer certain kinds of foreign consumer goods, and fill their homes with what were originally imitations of foreign furniture styles but which have long since assumed a uniquely Egyptian form. Foreign words are also commonly retained to name the items of foreign dress Egyptians now routinely wear as, for example, the *pullover, blusa,* and *jupe* (pronounced by substituting a *b* for a *p* in the spoken Arabic). Similarly in the middle classes, skirt lengths are referred to as *chanel* (just below the knee), *maxi* (ankle length), *mini* (above the knee), and *micro* (to the top of the thigh).

When all the classes travel abroad they bring back for themselves, and as gifts for others, consumer goods, materials, and items of clothing that people at home value almost as much for their foreign origins as for their usefulness

The generations:
rural sheikh with son
in government employ.

around the house. Foreign has recently come to mean more than something from outside the country in Egyptian society. Foreign connotes quality whether deserved or not. An Egyptian will often spend more for a foreign item rather than buy the Egyptian equivalent. Foreign has thus taken on the connotations of status and worth. There are complicated reasons for this phenomenon which we do not need to go into here.

Along with assuming middle-class educated status goes a new set of norms and standards of conduct for the socially mobile person coming from the lower classes. Middle-class women move more freely in public and work in bureaucratic jobs as a general practice. Women's office clothing does not, as in the West, move toward the adoption of more severely tailored (almost masculine) styles. Women

Folk and foreign styles: sheikhs and government officials in suit and "safari" outfit.

in Egypt emphasize their femininity—underlining the fact that though they are taking part in a "male" activity they have not lost their essential feminine attributes. Most women still tend to see their roles as more importantly involved in motherly and wifely tasks, and their employment as enhancing these roles by helping their families to afford more luxuries. Men still feel their role should primarily be one of economic supporter of the family. In order to preserve the separation of sex roles, many men insist that their wives' wages go for extras she wants rather than for basic family support.

Lower-class women who go to work are more bravely contradicting the norms of their class that until recently declared "shameful" any attempts to work outside the home by any but the most financially desperate women. Because the objection relates partly to the potential immoralities she may be exposed to, she may attempt to conceal her working activities from her neighbors, or alternatively promote a conservative demeanor by wearing even more modest clothing than is usual.[5] If she adopts foreign dress it will be of the most modest conservative kind. More likely if she is also educated she will don a form of Islamic dress

5. B. Ibrahim (1980) notes this tendency for women to wear more modest clothes when they undertake employment.

(see Chapter 7). Otherwise she will simply wear the typical lower-class dress with the full complement of modesty garments.

Lower-class women who switch too rapidly to middle-class dress may be accused of presumption as well as immorality as the following case illustrates:

> A. was left a widow with several small children. She is rumored to be a "bad" woman though there is nothing to prove that speculation. Several times she has told people that she is about to get married again but nothing happens, so people laugh at her and say she is trying to attract a man. This, they say, is why she puts on eye make-up and dresses in revealing Western clothes.
>
> She regularly attends a social religious service, held in a local welfare center, dressed in her "middle-class outfit": one time a tight black sweater and knee-length skirt, another time in a cast-off satin dinner dress with be-draggled cloth flower on the lapel. Her black stockings, befitting a widow's status, have large holes here and there that increase in size from week to week. When she enters the room, there is an audible titter of laughter, and the other women, who usually sit clustered together and touching, make a space for her to sit alone, as though she would contaminate them. She often makes a point of sitting on a bench rather than on the floor as most lower-class women prefer.
>
> She stresses also her brief education in a French nun's school by using occasional French words or by borrowing a hymn book and ostentatiously reading the Arabic, which most of the others are unable to do. Unfortunately, the women of the meeting know her as lower class and resent her efforts to put on airs. When they see her at home or in her immediate neighborhood, she wears typical lower-class dress and no make-up. People say she uses the meeting as an excuse to parade through the streets in her finery in hopes of attracting a rich merchant or skilled craftsman for a husband.

People accept a change in social class at the time a person is young, coming as a result of extended education, but later class changes for economic or other reasons are looked upon as presumptuous. For example, a person from the lower social classes who becomes affluent may expand his living space or the consumer goods he has available but he could not move to the neighborhoods of higher classes or suddenly assume foreign dress without risking the ridicule of all the people. Several popular Egyptian films have used such themes to poke fun at the topsy-turvy nature of modern life that, for example, gives a garbage collector more buying power than a university professor. This particular film devastatingly ridicules the garbage collector's attempts to assume a higher class life style including of course his tasteless use of foreign dress styles.

In sum, dress can provide a useful way of mediating a transition from one status to another. It can formalize a change in class so that individuals will be publicly treated with the courtesies that accompany that class. Or it can ease a change in roles, from housewife to working woman, by emphasizing the continuing respectability or femininity of the worker. Such a mediating role works well for dress if the new status is a legitimate one that people can understand is appropriate. But if they do not see other supporting evidence of legitimate changes in status, they look upon the change of dress as laughable. Often, it happens anyway that the understandings in dress marking fine distinctions of class are so subtle that they defy imitation by those outside the in-group.

WEALTH AND POVERTY

In Egypt wealth and poverty are found in all social classes. Foreign and folk dress both have markers that convey gradations of wealth. Folk dress shows wealth in at least five ways. First, through the costliness of materials. For men, the preferred expensive materials are fine wools and cottons; for women they are velvets, silks, and satins. High quality folk outfits of men and women can be extremely costly when the expense of materials, additional braids, and other decorative materials, and the expenses of tailors and dressmakers are added together. The poor wear muslins and cheap cottons. The rich wear leather slippers and shoes; the poor wear plastic slippers if they wear shoes at all. Secondly, the quantity and elaboration of materials used is often an indicator of wealth. The more a skirt or dress is gathered whether from a yoke or a waist, the greater the expense in materials and tailoring. The addition of ruffles is another way more material is used. Sometimes the very choice of more commodious modesty outfits made from expensive materials is a way of showing prosperity. Decorative materials increase the basic costs of dress considerably. For folk dress, these include piping, braid, beads, and sometimes sequins and for bedouin more embroidery and silver and gold coins.

Thirdly, people demonstrated wealth by variety in outfit—by differentiating everyday wear from best dress with outfits bought specifically for separate occasions and not designated for those occasions simply on the basis of the age of the dress. Fourth, financial capability is shown by the completeness of the full formal outfit with, for women, a presentable modesty covering, good shoes and possibly stockings and an elegant dress that is revealed by the movement of the modesty garment; for men, it includes good shoes and socks, a fine head cloth,[6] good quality galabiya, and sometimes an elegant shawl or cloak. Finally, the state of repair and cleanliness of the clothing indicates a person with enough extra resources to see that the proper attention to attire is taken. The folk generally dress as well as their financial resources permit. Excess resources are put into gold jewelry, another indicator of economic status.

6. Some people attribute the size of a Nubian male's white turban to his wealth.

Showing wealth through folk dress styles entails risks as well as rewards. The lower classes are always conscious of the precariousness of their financial resources, and are therefore adverse to "showing off" their affluence for fear of the "evil eye" and the jealousy of neighbors who may undermine their prosperity by natural or supernatural means. Flaunted wealth is one thing however, while wealth displayed at appropriate times is another, reflecting well on community as well as family reputation. Among the lower classes, a fat, healthy, well-dressed, gold-bespangled woman advertises her family as one with economic resources beyond the minimum needs for everyday life and, all other factors being satisfactory, her children are coveted as marriage partners.

> A widow, Um Fuad, lives alone in a lower-class neighborhood of Cairo. She has raised her children well, educating most of her boys so they now have moved off to middle-class jobs and neighborhoods. They keep her well supplied with clothing and conveniences, including an expensive cache of her favorite types of ground coffee. Her major social activity of the week is to attend a welfare center's general meeting on Wednesday mornings. There she dresses simply but neatly in her everyday modesty overdress and shawl. One day she let it be known at the meeting that she was ready to marry her youngest son, the more difficult of her children who had not taken to education, and thus had remained a simple vegetable peddler.
>
> One day a woman helping her with this matter arrived at the door to say she had made an appointment for Um Fuad to meet an eligible candidate. With deliberate haste, Um Fuad stripped down to her underwear, donned a lace-edged petticoat and over that a dark brown velvet dress of voluminous mass with ruffled flounce at bottom edge. Finally she covered the whole of this with a silk overdress and a velvet shawl. She arrived at the room where the girl lived to find her ill in bed with her hair uncombed, and looking generally unkempt. Um Fuad sat long enough to have tea with the girl and her mother but her displeasure was obvious. While making tea, the mother casually remarked as she left the door ajar, that the cupboard was filled with the accumulated clothing and bedding prepared for the young girl's marriage. Um Fuad could see the neat stacks of clothing: undergarments, dresses, nightgowns, etc. Soon after tea, Um Fuad swept out of the room and subsequently both sides said they rejected the other as potential marriage partners.

The meanings of this confrontation are not all clear. Um Fuad dressed in her best on this formal occasion to represent her family well (while in the weekly meeting she was careful not to overpower her poorer neighbors with displays of her affluence). She was rebuffed by the girl's poor appearance, which may have been genuinely a result of illness or on the other hand a rejection of the suitor who had a poor reputation in the quarter. Did the girl's mother show off the readied trousseau because she had second thoughts after seeing the impressively dressed Um Fuad or was she trying to convey the impression that they were after all people of substance, despite the poor appearance of the daughter on that particular day? Um Fuad's magnificence threw down a challenge that was difficult to meet without appearing eager to accept her son.

Some lip service is paid in Egypt to dressing without extravagance, no matter what the financial condition, but fundamentally most people believe that the wealthy will naturally display what they have. Status is too inextricably bound up in such public displays. A proverb, "Poverty is modesty and wealth leads to extravagance" sums up the inseparability of the condition and the action.

While the display of wealth may be a conscious choice, the display of poverty is usually more a result of circumstance. The poor operate in a world of hand-me-downs, charitable offerings, and the remaking of cast-off clothes. Those who can afford new material buy the subsidized cloth found in government stores. The cost in 1983 for a sturdy cotton was about 55¢ a meter (or 20¢ with a ration card). The price-conscious lower classes know well the limited range of designs and qualities of these materials. Though a woman may have an inexpensive everyday dress made from these materials, she advertises her poverty if she does not seek better material for a best dress. She wants, for the sake of her family's reputation, to look her best on formal occasions.

Few people intentionally set out to demonstrate their poverty, even when they are seriously strapped for funds. Sometimes, however, the ability to appear *miskiin* (pitiable) has important consequences for triggering increased goods and income from charitable neighbors or even strangers. A glance at the beggars lined up at the bridge entrance in Cairo shows the immediate advantage of appearance in eliciting contributions. One beggar, Ali, drives a car which he parks several blocks away from his favorite place. He dresses in the complete outfit of a woman, from granny dress to scarf or shawl. It is easy for people to imagine circumstances where women would have to beg, and even able-bodied ones are not expected to work. A tattered dress is enough to solicit aid. Men, however, usually have to show gross disability: age, blindness, missing limbs, or other deformities to elicit such support.

The display of wealth may have the opposite effect of placing greater social and economic obligation on the wearer. When saved for special occasions and for visits to neighboring towns, elegant dress reflects back positively on the village of the wearer and thus serves individual and community needs for recognition.

Foreign dress distinctions of wealth are subtle but just as comprehensible to in-groups of the elites as folk dress distinctions are to the lower classes. Elites demonstrate their wealth by adopting styles selectively based on conservative European tastes.[7] Cut, material, skilled tailoring, taste, and variety, skilled match-

7. This book is not concerned in any exhaustive way with the historical reasons behind Egyptian tastes. However, the turn to European styles came during the late nineteenth and early twentieth

ing of items of dress and other subtle distinctions are key clues to the old elites. Ostentatious expense and daring styles are more common among the new elites. Velvet, gold glittering fabrics, dramatic hairstyles, and extravagant jewelry are part of the inventory.

The current fad among some university-aged elites is jeans and even here there is a scramble to wear imported jeans with the proper designer names. There is no mistaking an elite's foreign-cut jeans for the locally made jeans that some middle-class students wear. The elites' ability to travel widely usually makes them more sophisticated in the use of foreign styles. Their use of the styles in air-conditioned homes and private cars makes more practical sense than in the difficult environments of the middle classes.

The use of such revealing styles as slacks among the higher classes, of course, is considered fashion whereas their use among the lower classes would, as Khuri notes, be immoral. Pants worn by a middle-class woman are also in many ways considered a presumption if the woman is thought to be imitating the upper class's presumed greater license. To prevent this impression, complicated definitions of modesty have to be drawn up to conform with middle-class values of modesty. Slacks have a double drawback: they reveal the whole of a woman's form, as well as the taboo area of the crotch which dress is intended to obscure. A hot argument grew up between one young man I knew and his fiancee, both university graduates, when he saw her bend over to pick something up so that her posterior was clearly visible to some young men standing nearby. He argued that if she was going to wear pants she should stoop by bending her knees and not by bending from the waist. The argument erupted again when she lifted a pant leg to show a medical doctor friend an infected mosquito bite.

Modesty and provocation are difficult areas to define with foreign dress and modern requirements. A young researcher on a trip with me once became ill. A doctor travelling with us prescribed a shot in her buttocks but her male cousin, also a researcher, refused to allow their colleague to administer the shot. An attempt to find a female nurse at a nearby hospital failed, and eventually the other female researchers took her to a male pharmacist, a stranger, where by artfully draping all areas they were able to expose only an inch or two of skin. (What a surprise later when the pharmacist proposed to an accompanying researcher— the only one of the group dressed in Islamic dress.)

A final anecdote about pants illustrates how this article of dress can be used to show sophistication. A young woman from a small town whose parents had died was visiting her aunt in Cairo. She was eager to marry and have her own home and her aunt was being helpful in finding suitors for her. A young man

---

centuries when relieved of Turkish domination and inspired by previous reforms of Mohammad Ali, Egyptians sought to build a society based on the model of Western democracies. The more intensive contacts with the West during that period contributed to the hastening of the influence.

and his mother appeared one day for a visit and after a suitable length of time, the young woman entered the room bringing refreshments. She had donned slacks thinking that this attire would make her provincial origins less noticeable. After the man returned home he sent word that he was uncertain about marrying the young woman because, among other reasons, he was unable to determine what her legs were like under the slacks. He said he would return for a second visit and he wanted her to wear a skirt. She went out with her aunt to buy a knee-length skirt, but even so when her suitor came again he rejected her because as he had expected "her legs were too thin."

One of the ways that Egyptian elite dress differs from European models is that it normally does not have much use for the informal casual wear that Europeans consider a basic part of their wardrobes. When jeans are worn, for example, they are worn as high fashion with high heels and silk shirts and not as leisure wear. One constraint on informality in upper-class styles is the fear of not being recognized as an elite. In Egyptian society, where elites are accorded special privileges even as strangers on the street, it is desirable to be recognized as elite and not wear the casual clothes that might cause confusion. Elites do, however, adopt modified versions of local folk galabiyas. It would be difficult to confuse these outfits with folk outfits; the cut (women wear a dress similar to the male folk galabiya) and the extravagant material and decorative braiding quite clearly mark them off as different.

The styles of the elites change more rapidly than those of the folk classes, partly because prestige demands a keeping up with reasonably modern styles. Lane's descriptions of elite fashions in the middle of the nineteenth century, for example, bear little resemblance to the elite styles of today while lower-class patterns still bear certain similarities to lower-class patterns of the period and even in some respects to former upper-class patterns (see Chapter 8).

We have spoken mainly of lower-class and elite clothing styles as most clearly defining class categories in Egypt. Middle-class styles seek to avoid any identification with lower-class groups and as far as possible to emulate the dress of higher classes without seeming to look presumptuous. The style which comes closest to being a truly middle-class style is Islamic dress (see Chapter 7), but even this dress is found in other classes. Individuals who wear Islamic dress would prefer to emphasize its religious rather than its class-related basis.

In recent years, the middle classes have increasingly come to be viewed as the impoverished classes because of their fixed, low, government salaries. Starting in 1979, the Ministries of Industry and Supply have exerted special efforts to produce large quantities of ready-made "foreign" clothing: suits, pajamas, shirts, and dresses. According to government sources, the decision to produce ready-made foreign clothes was taken to combat black-market dealing in cloth, to reduce imports in these items, and to bring down the soaring fees of tailors. It was hoped that Egypt would eventually be in a position to increase its own exports of such clothing. In 1980 government-produced woolen suits were available to the public at the price of £E35 (at that time a little more than $35) which compared with a tailor's price of about £E60.[8] Shirts produced in the public sector sold for about £E2. As was true of the government subsidized material, the locally produced clothing quickly became identified as products of low cost and often poor quality, to be shunned by those seeking to make a special impression.

At this point it is appropriate to draw the reader's attention briefly to the political implications of decisions about clothing styles and materials. The significant government decisions include the subsidization of prices for cloth used by the lower classes and middle classes, the banning of specific kinds of lower-class dress from certain educational institutions and extreme forms of Western dress from others (see Chapter 7), the requirement that children wear uniforms in school, and in some governorates that school girls wear scarves covering their hair. In all the instances above except the subsidization of cloth prices, government interventions concerning dress reflect the styles and views held most widely by the urban middle classes.

MALE-FEMALE IDENTITIES

Dull, solid colors, stripes, and occasionally plaids are considered appropriate for the folk dress of men; prints—especially flowered prints—and bright solids are appropriate for women (unless they wear black). Most of the time people tend to choose what is considered an appropriate color for their sex, just as most of the time a woman will not wear what is considered a man's galabiya. There are at least three circumstances, however, when women choose what is recognized as male dress. The first is a unique example—occurring in a population on the East bank of the Nile near the town of Balyana, little known except by river people who pass the area. The Beni Yahya, boatmen told me, are known for dressing their women in men's galabiyas and putting them to work in the fields like men. It is difficult, they say, to know they are women except at a close distance. One boatman told of how the Beni Yahya spent an hour or two helping him free his grounded boat and it was not until he had time to talk to them that he realized some were women dressed as men.

The few Beni Yahya women I saw, before they disappeared into the foliage of the banks of the river, wore striped, plain, or khaki-colored men's style galabiyas, and khaki scarves, some wound loosely around their heads in what could be taken for a men's style. Some women wore their head scarves tied under the

---

8. These comments, including prices, come from Mr. Talaat Yasin, Commercial Director of the Egyptian Company for the Purchase of Egyptian Products in a public announcement.

chin, not really a man's style, but also not typical of the way folk women in Egypt tie their scarves.

Beni Yahya children played on the sand banks in the same khaki galabiyas and mixture of head cloths tied either under the chin or thrown loosely over the head. The sex of the children was impossible to determine by their dress, but the women were identifiable by the plastic "shib-shib" slippers they wore.

It is difficult to know, without studying the Beni Yahya further, why they choose this style of dress. Are there distinguishing features of male and female dress that are not so apparent to an outsider? For some historical, economic, or defensive reasons was it useful to wear such dress (for any number of practical reasons or to confuse outsiders about the strength of the community)? On other trips through the area in 1984 and 1985 I saw the same styles and the same khaki-colored or striped galabiyas. From remarks of those with me, I felt that an important aspect of the "masculine" quality attributed to the dress by other Egyptians was the "unfeminine" nature of the color khaki or of striped fabric.[9]

Another place one finds "masculine" styles is among younger urban women of the lower social classes. They frequently wear a galabiya they call galabiya rigali (a "man-style" dress). The dress is not strictly speaking a male dress; it takes its name from its similarity to the closer cut galabiya frangi that men wear who are eager to show their greater sophistication. Symbolically the galabiya rigali may be considered the women's "sophisticate" equivalent of the men's galabiya frangi.

This style usually has a shirt style neckline with collar and button placket to below the waist. In the West we would call it a shirtwaist dress with no join at the waist. The shape is A-line and well-fitted around the bodice and natural waist. The skirt flares to ankle-length. The dress material may be print or plain and it may be covered by a moda modesty overdress or more likely a melaya wrap. The rigali style is much more revealing of the woman's figure and is therefore more frequently found among the young than those older women whose corpulent figures are not displayed as well, nor are they as comfortable in its close fitting cut.

This rigali style in many ways can be considered the "foreign" dress of the lower classes. It carries a certain status because it is modern and slightly daring. It includes features that are considered of foreign origin and its inspiration comes at least in part from the typical school uniform which has a fitted top (a mid-thigh-length tunic) and pants. The dress, in effect, is simply a lengthening of the tunic top. To call the dress "rigali" (men's) is certainly no more than a convenience since the fitted bodice and waist accentuate rather than conceal the feminine shape.

The third circumstance in which men's dress is assumed by women is a more

---

9. Frequently I found it the case that villagers, when talking disparagingly about neighboring settlements, referred to the women's attire or behavior as "masculine." For example, they might say, "Over there in that village, they let their women work in the fields like men."

overt attempt to signal that the woman wishes to be treated more like a man. Lower-class women who run formal businesses, like restaurants or shops, or who sell soft drinks at a street corner stand, frequently don men's style galabiyas in either the solid colors or stripes that are favored by men. The mature woman is addressed as *ma'alima* (the feminine equivalent of master craftsman or skilled worker, which by the system of inflated titles common in Egypt is appropriate for a small shop keeper). A ma'alima is accorded respect in keeping with her propertied status and her abilities as a merchant. She engages in verbal combat with her customers on a level that does not distinguish between males and females. She may even have her own gang of rowdies that support her side in arguments or help her carry out acts of patronage. In lower-class urban neighborhoods, aggressive personalities are accorded respect, partly because no one pushes them around, an occurrence that people of these areas feel happens too often to them.

By their male dress, female entrepreneurs signal their desire to suspend the expectations of accepted feminine conduct without losing respect and reputation. By wearing what is "unattractive" they signify that they are not intending to display their physical charms while engaging in public activity. Their loud, aggressive banter contrasts with the modest demeanor that attracts men. This behavior is similar to the way the Egyptian middle class can suspend certain expectations about women's roles when women have titles like "doctora," or come from backgrounds of sufficient social or economic status to allow them to take positions of authority. Overt signalling of a suspension of the rules preserves normal conduct from eroding exceptions. For the ma'alima, wearing men's dress means she can project an image that maintains respect for her in the community.

PERSONAL STATUS AND GENERATIONAL DIFFERENCES

The way in which dress elements are manipulated suggests at least four significant personal status categories for females: a sexless phase of very young childhood, unmarried young girls, married women, and older women and widows. The general symbolic oppositions are married — unmarried (or complete — incomplete), and youth — maturity, even though dress also marks internal gradations within these oppositions. A young unmarried woman, for example, dresses differently from an older unmarried woman. "Married" is the normal desirable state and "not yet married" a state of preparation and anticipation of as yet unrealized status. Widowhood usually reduces the woman's status again, with some degree of compensation coming from the attentiveness of children that are the fruit of the marriage.

Very young lower-class children are usually treated as sexless. The unisex short dresses of young children are said to be partly protective from the evil eye that has difficulty distinguishing, and thus harming, boy children; it is also practical

Rural girl in dress com-
mon to all areas of Egypt.

when children have not yet mastered their toilet skills. Gradually after mastering these skills, children begin to wear clothing appropriate to their sex. Until about ten, rural and urban children of the folk classes and their parents pay little attention to their appearance and clothing. Clothing rarely fits properly, faces and hands are left dirty, and hair uncombed. Unless parents take an interest, the child remains unkempt until the changes of puberty begin to make dramatic changes in physical appearance and the child begins to be absorbed by the question of appearance.

Young Unmarried Girls

Girls all over Egypt who do not wear a miniature version of the mature woman styles wear two-piece outfits that include pants and some kind of top. The two

Young girl in dress similar
to her mother's.

are of matching color unless the pants have been adopted as an undergarment
for a longer dress. The pants are usually straight-legged, roomy, and look like
pajama pants. In fact, the outfit is comparable to the men's sophisticate pajama
style but in the case of girls the top is much longer; the incidence of its use is
widespread in rural areas. The top may be a standard waisted dress, cut off just
below or at the knee, or it can be a fitted top that reaches to mid-thigh, below
the critical point of the crotch area which should not be visible.

In the uniform school girls wear, the outfit consists of shorter suit jackets
and pants. At home young girls usually wear light (white background), colorful
prints, usually of the popular government-subsidized kustor (heavy cotton) or
flannel in the winter and lighter weight cottons in the summer. Their heads are
covered by small, colored scarves, tarha veils, or brightly colored (orange, zigzag
combinations of red and green, etc.) shawls. Outermost modesty coverings are
not usually demanded of young girls until they are close to marriage age and

Young girls of Qena in Upper Egypt.

even then many visit towns and walk through cities without them. The galabiya rigali style is popular with young lower-class urban women.

The young girls' dress described above suits their needs in fairly exacting ways. It meets modesty demands, which are most critical at this time, by covering the girl's body completely; the pants even allow her freedom of movement without embarrassing display of her private parts. The dress of a young woman is almost always fitted to her shape in a way that allows her to show off her attributes to prospective bridegrooms who can be very exacting about a woman who is too thin or not comely in other ways. There seems a tacit acceptance of the fact that young women can reveal their graceful shapes more openly than married and older women who have retired from sexual competition. In short, young unmarried girls' dress serves the need for modesty while still revealing the "goods" that are available to a marriage partner.

Married Woman's Dress

A married woman normally starts marriage with a whole new set of clothes in styles more appropriate to married women. The change may be only in details,

Young girls of the North
Sinai bedouin.

more somber colors, a longer dress, more elaborate decorative additions, and more
formal modesty coverings worn in a more circumspect way that show she is interested in upholding the dignity of her new household. Married women may
also wear pants when it is cold but they are expected to know how to arrange
themselves so the modesty function of pants is not necessary. Some are apologetic
about the new style pajama pants which they say are very "masculine" and not
like the gathered, lace-edged bloomers that used to be worn.

Eventually unmarried women slip into the same patterns as married women
if their hopes of marriage dim, and finally they even begin to be addressed as
though they were married, with "Sitt" prefixed to their names. They never, how-

ever, are permitted the name "Mother of So and So (a child's name)" that women covet and which in Egypt carries a special sound of respect.

Older Women and Widows' Dress

Older women and widows[10] almost always dress completely in black. They usually ease into this pattern through mourning deaths among relatives and friends, a growing conservativism with age, and perhaps a growing lack of interest in the attractiveness of dress. If they have not already done so by the time they are widowed, women of all ages don black clothing at the time of their husbands' deaths and usually remain dressed in black for the rest of their lives. It is not normally expected that women will remarry unless they are very young and childless. Black represents both mourning and modesty, and since both are considered appropriate states for women, it is not always easy to separate individual motives for wearing the color.

It is also difficult to distinguish what it is in dress that represents marital status and what is simply a youth-maturity or modern-traditional distinction. The fitted shirtwaist (rigali) dress, for example, conforms with the pattern of unmarried girls wearing more shape-revealing clothes, yet at the same time, it is a style considered more modern and less traditional than the clothing of the girls' mothers. Young girls who are used to wearing the style may continue to do so after marriage.

Folk patterns are not stagnant even though they tend to be conservative and slow to change in general style for economic and practical reasons. Younger people often add novel details to the general style of a proven costume to feel they are up-to-date without challenging the norms of appropriateness. When these novel details catch on for a generation, they become the traditional pattern against which the next generation of young people contrast their own novelties. I observed several examples of age-level modifications between youth (modernity) and maturity (tradition).

Youth-Maturity (Modern-Traditional)

People continually incorporate new elements into folk dress. One of the most common now is the addition of a collar—a "foreign" element found in "modern" dress for men and women of both lower and educated classes. Older folk dress

10. The tendency for men to choose wives considerably younger than themselves, along with men's generally lower life expectancies, combine to leave unusually high numbers of widows in Egyptian society.

Age and youth in a Delta village.

never has collars. In a village near Tukh, in Kalubiya governorate older women wear collarless dresses with the shape of the neckline resembling a simplified Sharqiya dress—the pointed oval is outlined by two rows of piping with a third outlining the lower edge of the yoke.

By contrast, all the younger women in the village wear the moda style dress with an indented neckline and collar, and an edging of lace at the yoke edge. This, in effect, is a print housedress version of the urban sophisticate style. The village lies near the major north-south road between Cairo and Alexandria, and the inhabitants have extensive contacts with these urban centers.

In all of Boheira Province today, the older patterns of yoked embire "Boheira" style (see Chapter 3) and Alexandria style (featuring full gathered waisted

The generations near Tukh: older women wear V-necked yoked dresses, and the younger women wear "foreign" collars.

skirt and puffed sleeves) are being abandoned by the young unmarried and married women for *moda* (fashionable) styles like the *moda* yoked overdress or a waisted style called *cloche*.

This last style flares out from the waist seam with few if any tucks or darts. The sleeve also fits more snugly to the upper arm than in the Alexandria dress, but both dresses extend to about the same point just below the knee. To the uninitiated this second *moda* style is not easily distinguished from the Alexandria dress, though to the young women of Boheira it is as different as flared pants and tight pants are to an American teenager. They note the figure-hugging smoothness across the hips of the *moda* dress, and its reduced bulk across the shoulders. The skirt in this *cloche* style has several variations: one with material cut on the bias, called *iid w rigal* (literally "hand and foot"), one with a flare created by cutting two equal semi-circles, called *sh'af*, and a third, called the *qasat cloche*, which has center rectangular panels, fitted between bias-cut gores at the sides. The *sh'af* style is usually much fuller than the others.

Both yoked and waisted *moda* styles usually have a V-neckline and a modern foreign collar. In this Delta example of Boheira, it is interesting to see how

Village of Tukh, youth and maturity variations: Mature, right figure;
Youth, center figure; Mature variation, left figure.

in a province where traditional patterns have drawn from both yoked and waisted
older styles, the younger generation develops new styles that are only modifications of some of the details of the older dresses. Geographically they no longer
maintain a strict definition of "yoked" and "waisted" territories as in the past.
Rather one is more apt to see the waisted moda in the countryside and the yoked
moda in the town, regardless of former patterns.

In Upper Egypt generational contrasts are more typically observed in modesty garments. In a village south of Qena, for example, older women almost always wear the birda, typical of Qena. Many wear the rough wool versions found
in the village in the past, but rarely with the stripes that are characteristic further
north. Now many wear a birda of finer black wool that from a distance is barely
distinguishable from the hubbara of Luxor. Younger women of more sophistication in the village wear the melaya liff. Again, this village is conveniently situated
on the main road to Luxor where there are many opportunities for urban contact.

Older men in many villages tend to wear small crocheted cotton or knitted
wool skull caps even in the summer. Young men are more likely to go bare-headed
or to wear a carelessly wound scarf over the head without a base cap. This exemplifies the tendency in older men to dress somewhat more formally than younger men.

In lower-class districts of Cairo, there is a tendency for women's head coverings to differ by generation. Rules are far from invariable, however. Older women tend to wear heavy, opaque coverings that conceal all the hair, and often the shoulders and entire neck area. Middle-aged women wrap lighter-weight, transparent black veiling a number of times around their heads to effect the same degree of hair cover as the older women. Young women may wear colored scarves with glimpses of hair showing underneath, and sometimes a twist of transparent veiling over the scarf but showing its color underneath. The veiling drifts down the back of the wearer. The variety in head coverings thus ranges from strict covering of all the hair to ever more carelessness about how much hair is exposed. Yet at no time does a lower-class urban woman leave her hair fully exposed as middle-class women do almost invariably, unless, of course, they wear the heavy coverings of the fundamentalist styles.

As noted above, using subtle differences to mark the up-to-date style of the young girl from her mother conveniently allows the girl to feel part of her peer group without challenging her mother's standards. There is more general sympathy between daughters and mothers in Egyptian society than between peers. One Egyptian observed that this was because mother and daughter know that someday they must be parted when the girl goes to her new home. In anticipation of this event and from the bond that develops in their common role, a sense of mutual solidarity grows between them. A girl takes her model for her future goals much more from her mother than she does from school or peer groups.

With the advent of greatly improved communication systems young people easily become familiar with new trends in dress. Though they usually do not choose to wear patterns that are totally different from those prevalent in their communities, many want to show that they know what is up-to-date in folk styles. Cities are the best locations to see new models, because they tend to gather together a variety of Egyptians from all over the country as well as from rural hinterlands. Styles that become prominently associated with urban life are appealing to country people who increasingly come to value things urban. Television also presents middle-class dress models to a widespread audience. Where folk dress styles are concerned, television almost always portrays outmoded styles or inaccurate representations of folk styles that are generated out of the imaginations of the middle-class programers of serials and other dramatizations.

MODESTY

In general modesty codes are more strictly directed at women who have the power to dishonor the family by their actual or presumed actions. Many writers have discussed the question of honor in Arab society. One who specifically deals with modesty and dress says: "The modesty code rests on two contradictory assumptions: that woman is weak and needs to be protected from threats to her honor and that she has strong sexual impulses which threaten the honor of males and the integration of group" (Maklouf 1979:38).

She notes that modesty garments protect women from males, and conversely protect society from the potentially disruptive power of women. In Egypt contemporary modesty requirements are not as strict as they are in the Arabian Peninsula, nor as they were among Egyptians of the higher classes at the beginning of the century. Referring to such contexts, another writer comments, "If women are secluded in a world behind walls and veils, men are excluded from knowledge of or control over the inner sanctum and yet are deeply affected by what occurs therein" (Webster 1984:256). She also notes wisely: "To view *harim* and *hijab* as conventions which seclude women from society is to contend that society consists of the male/public sphere, and that the female/private sphere is somehow peripheral to 'society.' Yet in reality, society is composed of both public and private spheres" (Webster 1984:256). I would argue the case more strongly and say that in the Arab world the private sphere takes on a value more closely approximating the value of the public sphere in Western society. Egyptian feminists fight for stronger rights in the family rather than in the public sphere where they are already protected with legal safeguards for employment and financial rights. By controlling much of what goes on in the family, women possess greater power in the Arab world than their seclusion would suggest.

With their vestigial modesty outfits, the folk women in Egypt have what, in many ways, is the best of both worlds. They may move with reasonable freedom in public areas while excluding certain males and outsiders from their private spaces. At the same time, with artful use, the garments convey a full range of subtle meanings and conceal as many imperfections as a girl may want to hide. I have rarely heard complaints against modesty garments even in their most opaque forms, and then usually from women who have spent some time abroad.

In Egypt, except for the fundamentalists, the veil is past history now. It was considered a momentous event in the history of the Egyptian feminist movement during the 1920s when Hoda Sharawi removed her veil in public, and like-minded women followed her example. She did not, however, throw out with the veil the definitions of public and private space or the essential definitions of women's roles. The veil, as symbol, was replaced by other symbols that preserved the fundamental complementarity of sex roles. Sharawi was able to challenge convention partly because she had a secure position among the upper classes. In many ways she was nothing more than a trend setter, and were it not for her strong feelings on the subject of women's rights, she would be considered as such.

Modesty garments, as other forms of dress, serve to distinguish gradations of social status and wealth, particularly at present among the lower classes. Rural women who use these garments sparingly because they interfere with field or house work are the first to make more use of them when family affluence permits help in these chores. They recognize the need for leisure and higher income to take full advantage of more complicated methods of "protection." On formal occasions modesty garments are more visible than other clothes and thus the quality of cloth and cut more open to scrutiny and assessment of the financial position of the wearer.

Modesty garments are symbolic in the sense that they mark people's intentions about moral issues. They are not covers intended to make women unrecognizable or unfeminine. To the contrary, they emphasize femininity, and by covering the imperfections allow the imagination free play to conjure up the most alluring possibilities underneath. The garments themselves offer endless opportunities for the wearer to adjust, drop, tighten, or loosen—in short, to make active use of all the symbolic and other potential meanings of such gestures. Where parents want truly to exert control, therefore, they rely on other, more secure, methods of protection, such as restricting the movements of women, sending along companions to accompany them, or in the most extreme cases performing the common operation of female circumcision.

Modesty is seen as performing a critical function because of its connection with the most significant event of Egyptian life, marriage. It provides the stage and the props by which many of the illusions surrounding that institution are created: virginity, beauty, good character, protection, and honor. Modesty garments provide the illusion if not the reality that a young woman is pure and moral in character—just the kind that a young man hopes to marry.

Egyptians are usually not dogmatic in their rules of behavior. They value modesty in principle but do not usually prescribe the exact acts that are required to produce modest behavior. For folk Egyptians, the contrast is often drawn between modesty (as a requisite of reputation), and provocation (as an inciter to immoral behavior). Individual determinations of the levels of physical attractiveness to reveal are usually left to family authorities to decide. There they are based on the standards of modesty that will create a desirable public image.

In general, people believe a woman's body should be largely covered, but a middle-class woman with her hair, legs, and arms revealed may feel herself as modest as the entirely veiled middle-class fundamentalist student. The significant dimensions for all classes are skirt and sleeve lengths, head coverings, and the tightness or looseness of fit. Most Egyptians would agree that it is the licentious intent to display the feminine charms that is provocative, but few would agree on precisely what the thresholds of licentiousness are. A convincing pretense of innocence is as good as the genuine article as far as a public audience is concerned.

One problem is that the ideas of appropriateness vary both between and within classes. A lower-class woman exposing her breasts to nurse a baby for example, is only confirming her valued role as mother, and is not seen as advertising her sexuality. A higher-class mother carries out such functions in the privacy of her home.

Modesty as Symbol

These days in Aswan it is not uncommon to see a vivid example of modesty coverings reduced to their symbolic essence — young, educated Nubian girls dressed in foreign dress with skirts reaching to just below the knee, and covered with a fully transparent modesty garment, the jirjara. With this see-through modesty outfit, the young woman displays her educated status — her modern outlook — while reminding people that she remains essentially a modest young woman, a worthy choice as a marriage partner.

In the folk classes one finds with increasing frequency these days, waisted and yoked modesty overdresses made up in transparent versions of net or lightweight material. Sometimes the raised velvet of flower patterns makes the garment slightly less transparent. For a time these garments appeared so rarely that they seemed hardly worth mentioning but now they appear with enough regularity to suggest a new moda fashion warranting remark. The style supplies another example of the trend toward lighter garments with fewer layers in the heat of summer, while still respecting the letter, if not the complete spirit of modesty norms.

Modesty garments are often put to other uses than strict modesty functions.

Modesty as Convenience

In a study of young women in Christian Akhmiim, Fahmy notes that the women often went about town on everyday errands shrouded in a birda cloak to cover their house dresses. On Sundays, however, when they were dressed in their best finery to go to mass, or when they went to the nearby city of Sohag, they appeared in public areas without modesty garments in order to be seen in their finery. All the young women associated the wearing of the birda with poverty. It allows a poor woman to preserve a proper appearance when her everyday clothes are not as presentable as she would like. (Fahmy 1979:50)

Fahmy notes the similarity between the word for the kind of cloak found near Sohag, the birda, and the Indian word "purdah" meaning seclusion. (However, see Chapter 3 for what is probably a more accurate derivation for the word.) Most of the young women she studied wore the birda at one time or another. Girls said they had to wear it when they approached marriageable age, especially after their elder sisters married and they were considered next in line to marry.

If the elder sisters remained unmarried, they eventually discarded the birda so they would not look like adolescent girls. Girls who received an extended education never wore the birda and, as they grew older, donned either foreign dress or if they were Muslims, sometimes Islamic dress (see Chapter 7). While Akhmiim, as an adjunct village of Sohag, may not be representative of the majority of small villages in Egypt, it has enough features in common so that some of its practices are not unusual. The use of modesty covers for purposes of hiding clothing that is not publicly presentable is one of these widespread practices.

Modesty is situational even for those who maintain fairly strict standards. In the house, form-concealing night clothes are appropriate even when guests drop in unexpectedly. Outside the house, a woman dresses more circumspectly according to her family's and her community's sense of what constitutes private and public space.

Modesty as Definer of Space

In urban areas, women frequently don a modesty garment the moment they walk over their thresholds into the street. In small villages women may walk the length of populated areas without wearing such garments. They wear their modesty garments, along with their best clothes, when they visit a nearby town. In other villages, women may go without modesty garments only in the vicinity of their homes, and wear them to collect water from the Nile, or to work in the fields. In general, women frequently feel compelled to wear modesty garments when among strangers—strangers meaning in some cases non-relatives. Along the Nile, especially in Upper Egypt, the incidence of outermost modesty garments rises dramatically as one approaches major towns and cities where the chance of meeting strangers increases.

Another way a girl can use modesty garments as a definer of social space is seen when she wants to indicate that certain males might be considered eligible marriage partners for her. This of course happens at puberty in a general way toward all stranger males, but it might happen in a more specific way when she suddenly decides a male cousin should no longer see her quite so informally. Staying out of his way or coyly covering her mouth with a corner of her tarha brings home to him, better than any other way, the possibilities for marriage that exist. On the other hand, a more determined withdrawal and heavier cover may mean just the opposite, a determination not to marry this particular person. The titillation comes in never being completely sure of which message is being sent.

A wearer may decide to use some show of modesty also when the space that she enters situationally becomes defined as questionable. For example, a middle-class woman who must go out at night may cover her head with a scarf, not her usual habit, in order to define her activity as respectable.

Young women showing off their attractions at the well (Lower Egypt).

Men's and women's folk dress covers the body to approximately the same degree, even though the strictures about women's modesty are stricter. If the situation demands it, men may undress completely, as for example when a man takes his water buffalo to the Nile for a bath. Women never take off more than the outer modesty garments even when work makes it inconvenient for them to be so heavily dressed. A woman washing clothes in the canal may put aside a cloak with dragging hems or sleeves, or she may hitch her clothing to her knees to bend to fill her water jug from the river, but that is the limit of her undress. It is not surprising, knowing this, to see why women tourists in shorts or sleeveless dresses create such a stir in Egypt where such outfits are tantamount to advanced stages of undress.

For women, the important distinction in dress relates to levels of modesty in public and private space; for men, the significant distinction is the level of formality in dress. Daily life and work is informal, requiring garb that is functional and does not hinder activity. Special events, visits, and travel to the city, require different levels of formality, up to and including a man's newest and best set of clothing. Men's folk dress for formal occasions normally includes besides a complete outfit of clothing, a suitably fine headdress, which remains on his head at all times of the visit. For a man as for a woman, moving into public space requires that consideration be given to the public image the person, and indirectly the person's family, creates. Part of a man's formal demeanor is the requirement that a proper man behave with some modesty toward women. He should not stare at them or linger overly long speaking to them. A man should loudly announce his presence before entering a private home and if he should come upon women inappropriately attired, he should avert his eyes.

Women's modesty garments symbolize two opposing states, one in which the "goods" which are concealed are worth hiding and discovering — the case of a woman ready for procreation, for example — and the second, where a woman has withdrawn from the competition of the sexual market place because she has married or because her sexual functions have come to an end, in old age or widowhood. The first is of course a more titillating stage, enhanced if anything by the manipulative possibilities of modesty garments. Modesty garments may, of course, be used with the opposite effect for which they are ostensibly intended. While they allow the wearer to follow the letter of the rules of cover, they may be arranged consciously or unconsciously in a way that provokes attention. The example of the clinging melaya liff has been given above. This garment draws the folds of clothing to the body and remains all the more seductive because of what is left to the imagination. A prospective groom needs his appetite whetted but will refuse to touch what carries even the faintest taint of marred reputation.

For married women who are still physically attractive, social pressures encourage circumspection in dress without any of the seductive "silliness" that is accepted as part of a young girl's behavior. The young to middle-aged married woman is at the most active phase of her life and she should have no time for distracting activities. She wears the standard costume, which is designed to accommodate her activities, and should not spend much thought on enhancing her appearance. Nevertheless, she is recognized as still in the years of procreation and thus represents a potential danger to family and community honor. A straightforward preoccupation with housework is considered the most appropriate way for her to be engaged.

Older women in their heavy modesty outfits are not so much fearful of advances as they are desirous of retiring from the fray. As they grow older, their retirement from sexual competition is recognized by a growing acceptance of their presence in discussion circles with men. Their use of heavy modesty covers comes from a long acquaintance with the garments and perhaps from the warmth such garments bring to arthritic bones — as much practical reasons as symbolic ones.

The outside observer cannot fail to note the contradictions that arise between what people say is the intent of modesty styles and what can be actually observed from people's use of them. First, modesty garments rarely conceal more of the flesh than is already covered by clothing worn underneath. It is true that they may obscure the shape to greater degree and they cover the hair and neck area more completely in some cases. The fact that they are generally black complies with the Islamic precept that women not draw attention to themselves in a provocative way. It is unlikely, however, that it is for this reason that women wear black, since much of folk dress is brightly colored and wholly black outfits are found more commonly among the old and bereaved. The fact that modesty garments do little to conceal the figure beyond what is already accomplished by ordinary dress suggests that these garments should be considered more as symbols of modesty and morality rather than as guarantors of that morality.

A similar contradiction exists in the fact that the more conservative areas of Upper Egypt possess dress styles that in general waisted form are more figure revealing than the granny styles of more liberal Lower Egypt. In large areas of Upper Egypt women also wear relatively shorter length skirts and the abbreviated modesty wrap, the shawl.

A third contradiction is found in the fact that though young girls and young unmarried women are at the most sexually vulnerable time of their lives, their styles are almost invariably more form-fitting than those of married and older women, and their modesty coverings more revealing because of their lighter-weight materials and their less well-anchored styling. The heaviest opaque modesty covers are reserved most frequently for older women past their childbearing years.

Women wear modesty covers ostensibly so they will be shielded from the view of "stranger" men whom they are eligible to marry. Yet modesty covers no longer, except in the most extreme cases of Islamic dress, conceal a woman's face or even much of her bodily outline. In addition, a woman going to the fields or to collect water, rarely covers except in deeply conservative areas, so that the most eligible men, those from the village, and even more likely, her father's brother's sons have many opportunities to view her.

One way to look at the regional contradictions is to theorize that different dynamics affect the country's areas at different speeds and with different results. For example, traditionally conservative Upper Egypt, remote from the new conservativism of cities like Cairo, may be moving away from heavy reliance on dress styles to serve the modesty function. Modesty covers still symbolize the state of mind and the essentials of the modesty codes. The fact that lip service in this area is given to claims that women remain close to home and do not work in the fields or visit cities, despite a great deal of evidence to the contrary, suggests that families consider the restriction of a woman's movements as the most effective form of control. Such sayings as "Under the veil there is lethal poison," demonstrate the lack of confidence in purely formal kinds of cover.

Lower Egypt, in the Delta area, has always been quicker to adopt the trends coming out of Cairo. Except in remotely rural parts of the Delta, the granny style overdress modesty robe is widely accepted. This style is in keeping with more conservative modesty codes coming out of urban areas. Though less rigorous and less tied to religious rationales among the lower classes than among the middle class in urban areas, the trends are nevertheless important. The dress of younger lower-class married women has tended to become brighter, lighter weight, and more revealing of the hair without in most cases revealing the bodily shape any more distinctly. When compared with middle-class fundamentalist styles, these lower-class styles show an inattention to the stricter interpretations of Islamic dress requirements that ask for more sober colors, opaque materials, and a complete concealment of the hair. The middle classes usually claim that the lower classes are ignorant of religious meanings and implications even though they may comply with some of the formal requirements of Islam. The next chapter deals more thoroughly with the issues of dress and religion in Egypt.

The final contradiction, with regard to the more revealing styles of the vulnerable young women, may have a functional explanation. In the context of today's marriage patterns where individuals are more likely to make their own choices of spouses, albeit from a distance, it behooves young women in public to present as appealing and attractive an appearance as possible. Fitted dresses and bright colors, a shy demeanor, and industrious, sensible attention to tasks at hand, graceful adjustment of drapes and scarves, are all irresistible inducements to the romantically inclined young man. Parents are aware of the need to "sell" their daughters in this way, and are willingly implicated in the plot, while speaking openly only of modesty and control. Indeed there is a thin line that a girl must walk between revealing too much or concealing too much.

The basic tension affecting individual choices rests with decisions about what to conceal and what to reveal in the psychological, social, and physical sense. Revealing and concealing can be actions that physically cover or uncover parts of the human body. Or they can be actions that convey, clarify, distort, or obscure the intentions of the wearer. Emphasis in Egypt is usually not placed on originality or individuality in dress. Rather, if these characteristics occur at all they are more likely to result from personal interpretations of conformity to group norms. People in Egypt receive their strength from primary groups and thus have no reluctance to show their identification with them.

Religion and Dress

"Wash him and wind a turban around his head." He replied, "Am I both washer and guarantor of entry into Heaven?"[1] —Arab proverb

PIETY

MODESTY NORMS receive much of their strength from the moral underpinnings of religious authority that people believe support them. That being said, it is also important to note that even when there are authoritative religious texts that are relevant, the interpretation of what constitutes modesty by religious standards varies widely. The Muslim religion places greater stock in a person's intentions than in actual conformity to specific sets of rules. Religious texts set fairly broad statements of principle regarding modesty, while the social sub-group defines the way principles should be interpreted and executed. Whether a person follows the sub-group's codes or not, he or she will be generally aware of the implications in the eyes of others of wearing certain kinds of dress.

Increasingly since 1967, a new Islamic style of dress has appeared on the streets of major cities in Egypt. In some cases the dress indicates the wearer's more fundamentalist view of religion; in others it is worn more as the latest fashion, *akhir moda*. In this second group, the same girls who several years ago might have worn a mini-skirt as the latest fashion adopt more modest styles now because they have become popular. A study carried out by the National Centre for Social and Criminological Studies found that more than sixty percent of their sample of educated Egyptian women wear Islamic dress. Of these, forty percent claim they wear it for reasons of modesty and cost, twenty-five percent because it is fashionable, ten percent to avoid going to a hair dresser, and five percent because they feel that men are less likely to molest a modestly dressed woman.

---

1. The speaker is talking about a corpse. In this case the turban is being referred to as a sign of piety.

Islamic dress: Fundamentalist styles, right 2 figures; pious styles, left 2 figures.

Women's Islamic Dress (*zey islami* or *zey shari'a*)

The standard fundamentalist dress consists of an ankle-length robe (*gilbab*) flowing from the shoulder, with long sleeves and high neckline. It is made from a fairly heavy material, cotton or wool, in single colors of subdued hues, brown, blue, grey. A head covering (*khimara*) of medium-weight material in white or a subdued color is adjusted low on the forehead to cover effectively every trace of the hair, and circle the oval of the face, concealing the neck area as well. This head covering resembles the wimple used by nuns in the Western world.

The costume may be composed of these two parts or in cases of extreme piety, the woman may add gloves, a full face veil (niqab) with cutouts for the eyes, and even sometimes sunglasses to cover the eyes. (The terms gilbab, khimara, and niqab are all general terms used by the bedouin of the Middle East, especially in Saudi Arabia, to refer to similar but not identical items of dress.) This dress conforms maximally with fundamentalist interpretations of religious

Three versions of fundamentalist dress and one foreign dress.

injunctions that the modest woman's body should be covered, her clothes loose-fitting, and her hair concealed.

This extreme form of fundamentalist dress interprets the Koranic language, "And if you ask his (the Prophet's) wives for any object, then ask them from behind a curtain (*hijab*); that is purer for your hearts and theirs" (33:52), as meaning "from behind a veil." The head covering or veil of the fundamentalist costume is also called *higab* (the colloquial of hijab). This costume reflects religious piety. The more the wearer is covered, the more she demonstrates her piety. Some say that there are definite gradations[2] of the dress that women consider carefully before increasing the level of their commitment.

A second pious, but not necessarily fundamentalist, outfit is fitted or waisted

2. Some fundamentalists measure piety in three grades that incorporate the two standard styles of Islamic dress. In the first, the hair is well covered, the dress long or short and waisted. In the second, the dress is long and loose and the neck is definitely covered. In the final stage, the woman is veiled completely and she wears gloves.

(usually composed of skirt and blouse) and ankle-length. It may be worn in sub-dued colors but sometimes part or all of the outfit is brightly colored or even patterned. The head cover may consist of a scarf twisted turban style that bares the neck area but covers the hair, or it may consist of a knit or crocheted wool or cotton helmet (*bonné*) that fits snugly over the head and fans out to cover the neck, breast, and shoulders. In the 1980s an attractive addition to more snugly fitting headdresses is what appears to be a circlet of rope anchoring the cloth at the crown of the head. The "rope" is formed by twisting colored ribbons loosely with the long ends of the head scarf and wrapping these around the head in a band of alternating stripes of ribbon and head cloth. This second version of pious outfit differs from the first in that the physical form of the wearer is revealed from head to toe, and there is greater freedom in the use of colors and, in some styles, in showing the neck areas.

One wearer of this style commented that the Koran says ". . . the women of the believers (should) draw their cloaks round them (when they go abroad). That will be better so they may be recognized and not annoyed" (Sura 33:59). She interpreted this verse to mean that women's dress should not conceal a woman so much that she cannot be recognized personally as a good and moral woman.

Young women who consider themselves pious wear a number of variations of these two standard styles, manipulating the elements of the dress in ways that suit their own interpretations of Islamic injunction. Implied in their explanations of why they wear a particular style is their belief that they have chosen what is the "correct" Muslim dress—that is, they speak in terms of religious rather than secular rationales if they feel called upon to explain themselves.

The two standard versions of Islamic dress indicate some of the differences in the way Koranic verses may be interpreted even by those who consider themselves pious and want to express their piety in dress. Even established religious authorities are wary of stating the specific requirements of modesty attire too dogmatically. In February 1981, Al-Azhar University Dean al-Naggar required Islamic dress for girl students but did not define what it should constitute, only noting that blue jeans and tight skirts were not appropriate. A journalist, Ahmed Bahget, in a column in *Al-Ahram* (January 14, 1980) quotes Sheikh Mawdoudi as saying that a truly devout woman who is keen to guard her chastity should not be subjected to specific constraints. On her own, she will not display parts of her body in order to attract men.

The Muslim Students' Association of the U.S. and Canada publishes a pamphlet on appropriate Muslim woman's dress. It identifies four requirements that must be observed according to the Koran. The first concerns the extent of covering: the entire body must be covered except for specifically exempted areas which are held to be the face and hands and whatever appears inadvertently through uncontrollable factors such as the wind blowing a garment, or a woman caught unaware by the presence of someone who should not see her. Second, the dress should be loose enough so as not to reveal the shape of a woman's body or, preferably, a cloak may be worn to cover a more form-fitting garment. Third, the cloth of the garment should be thick enough so as not to show the color of the underlying skin or the details of the body. Finally, the overall appearance should be decorous and not designed to attract male attention. In addition, points that may vary with time and location but are clearly spelled out, according to this pamphlet, are that woman's dress not be similar to men's dress, nor to the dress of unbelievers, nor designed to show status, whether it be excessively rich or poor.

The basic requirements of Muslim woman's dress apply also to Muslim men's clothing with only a difference in degree. While the *awrah* (parts of the body that are covered at all times unless there is a specific exception) of women includes the whole body except the face and hands, the awrah of a man consists of the area between the navel and the knees (jurists differ on whether the knees and the thighs should be both included). Given the difference in awrah, the clothing of a male is still expected to cover the awrah, be loose, thick, and designed not to attract attention. It should not be similar to woman's clothes, to the dress of unbelievers, or worn for reasons of vanity or pride. In addition men should not wear silk or gold.[3]

It is not surprising that in recent years there has been a reactive swing in dress styles to a more conservative pattern, given the way that Western dress accentuates or exposes parts of the body that, by Muslim standards, should be hidden. The justification for style changes in Egypt, more than any other single factor, is the changing interpretation of what constitutes the religiously defined appropriateness of dress for males and particularly for females.

Men's Islamic Dress

The distinguishing feature of a fundamentalist perspective in men, more often than an item of dress, is likely to be a characteristically clipped beard with clean shaven cheeks and a narrow rim of hair outlining the jawline. Men have adopted the folk galabiya as the garb for the most pious of their members, in concert with the belief that men as well as women should not wear tight, form-revealing clothes.[4] A man who for some reason cannot wear the galabiya may substitute baggy pants. Because some administrators disapprove of folk styles for the educated, men have not taken to these styles in such great numbers as women,

3. Badawi, Jamal A. "Muslim Woman's Dress." Published by the MSA Woman's Committee of the Muslim Students' Association of the U.S. and Canada. Plainfield, Indiana.
4. One man said that technically a man should be covered from waist to about knee level, but even in such attire he should not come into the presence of women, as for example, when he is swimming.

whose fundamentalist dress is different enough from folk styles to make it suitable, or at least permissible.

When a university student adopts a folk galabiya, he sets up ambiguous signals that cannot always be accurately interpreted by his audience. On the one hand, his appearance in the galabiya does not indicate his valued educated status, and on the other, his piety is not unequivocally apparent. For the male fundamentalist there must be a certain amount of conflict inherent in donning a folk dress which does not convey clearly his state of mind to public audiences.

Most Egyptians would agree that the Islamic style originated with the university students after the demoralizing defeat by Israel in 1967 and received impetus from what were considered the successes of 1973. The 1967 defeat was attributed to the laxity in moral standards of Egyptians—a just punishment by Allah—while 1973 was considered a return of God's support after a tightening of moral standards. Many believed that without a return to religious values and conduct based on Islamic values there would be further failures for Egypt. Whatever its origins, the dress serves a number of latent and manifest functions, all of which have been noted at one time or another by observers of the contemporary scene in Egypt.

The dress allows a form of generational rebellion, by young people against the often liberal, pro-Western, middle-class attitudes of their parents. It is difficult for parents to criticize the new trends because of their religious overtones. For socially mobile children of lower-class parents who still maintain more traditional values, the dress provides a transitional outfit, less startling than other middle-class styles, but still signalling the acquisition of educated status for the young woman. The dress reflects a rejection as well of foreign remedies to Egyptian social and economic problems, and a new perspective that seeks solutions to problems in indigenous formulae and religious values.

Practically, the dress helps to alleviate some of the problems of contemporary Egyptian life. The dress cuts down on the costs[5] of a varied foreign wardrobe and the expense of hair dressers. The colors are practical, and the form-concealing style is considered protective of women who need to move about in public more freely as a result of extended education and employment.

With educated couples expected to take a greater part in selecting their own mates, Islamic dress is a way of narrowing the field of candidates so that at a glance on the big anonymous campuses, a man can determine a girl's piety and potential suitability for marriage. The behavior of a young woman who stops to speak with a young man is more apt to be construed positively if she is dressed in the Islamic style, according to this argument. Dress of course does not guarantee the piety of its wearer or even her morality, as critics of the style like to point out.

---

5. The Islamic outfit is often available through Islamic societies and mosques at a subsidized price of about $10–12.

What is perhaps the most interesting aspect of the fundamentalist style is the amount of thought that many wearers say they invest in the decision to wear the dress, and the strong feelings it generates in its proponents and opponents.

Islamic fundamentalist dress, for the most part, is a middle-class phenomenon. Although lower-class women wear folk dress styles that essentially accomplish the same modesty aims as either basic form of Islamic dress above, their motives are more related to community norms than to pretensions of piety. Lower-class women may be conscious of certain kinds of dress as appropriate for Muslims, but they are usually vague about both the specific items of dress that are required and the Koranic verses upon which requirements may be based. The elements of Islamic dress are selected in a way that makes the style unmistakably different from folk dress. Just as earlier veiling and now foreign dress serve to mark class distinctions, so Islamic dress serves to distinguish between educated and uneducated classes. As a consequence, foreign and Islamic dress have come to be the main alternative choices available to women of the educated middle and upper classes to mark their social status.

Fundamentalists would reject some of the latent secular functions an outside observer would find in Islamic dress. They prefer to see the dress as a sign of dedication to religious principles. Other thoughtful Egyptians who do not wear the dress put the trend in historical perspective. One young woman in her late 20s commented that her mother disapproved of the dress because she remembered seeing her own mother veiled and felt her own generation's adoption of foreign dress was an escape from the oppressiveness of an earlier time. The speaker had followed her mother's example in dress. Times were difficult when she and her friends were going to school, and they felt it a treat to have nice clothes like young people in the rest of the world. Now, with economic conditions somewhat better, girls like her sister, who is five years younger, view taking up Islamic dress as a choice that reflects their religious principles. They do not know veiling from before and do not feel that a return to wearing conservative clothes is oppressive because they have chosen it freely for themselves.

The speaker's comments help to explain some of the reasons that, according to many observers, mothers tend to be the most resistant to their daughters donning Islamic garb. Fathers tend to accept the styles more readily, at least partly because they feel it makes easier their task of maintaining the good reputations of their daughters before they marry. In other words, many people consider the dress public evidence that a girl has internalized and accepted self-controls about her modesty; whether this is indeed true may be less important to such people than the acceptable public image the girl presents.

In at least one case, Islamic dress styles have spilled over into styles for special occasions. The women's team of the Egyptian Volleyball Association created new Islamic sports outfits of trousers and closefitting headdresses to prove, they said, that Islamic dress need not hamper proper exercise. One player noted that they wanted the audience to come for the spectacle of the game and not for the spectacle of female bodies inappropriately exposed.

Islamic dress is not a turning back. The style is new, even though it incorporates elements of old styles. It exists in, and responds to, a whole new set of conditions in Egyptian society. In many ways the fundamentalist perspective recognizes that women in contemporary Egypt may need to appear more frequently in public areas than before, and gives them clothing that permits more decorous movement there. At the same time, the fundamentalist movement reasserts the complementarity of sex roles, and the special and preferred place of women in their roles as wives and mothers. The dress recognizes that fully feminine quality of women that, according to Islamic precepts, requires protection.

One scholar sums up the feelings of both schools of thought about fundamentalist and other kinds of Islamic dress when she notes:

> The present resurgence of Muslim garb for women is dismissed by cynics as a means for receiving a scholarship from funds allocated specifically for that purpose by conservative forces in the Arab world. While it might be true, this does not take away from the fact that young people appear to be responding favorably to the invitation to return to the roots of their heritage. This is done not only as a defense against what they see as the immorality and decadence of Western culture patterns, but to appropriate anew God's guidance for family life in order to build a strong united nation committed to the ideology of Islam as the only road of salvation for the world. (Haddad 1982:70)

From my own conversations with those wearing even the modified forms of fundamentalist dress, I would be reluctant to underestimate the strength of piety that underlies its use.

CHRISTIAN-MUSLIM

Historically, periods have varied in the extent to which people have signalled or obscured their religious identities. Usually it is not as necessary to mark explicitly the religion of the majority unless a frenzy of piety imbues religious symbols for a time with special meaning. Newcomers are assumed to be of the majority religion unless proven otherwise. In Egypt, Christians have often used this fact to their advantage.

For Christians, the question of whether to reveal their religious identity to strangers is complicated by social and economic as well as religious factors. At times it is an advantage and at other times it is not. As a minority group (from seven to perhaps ten percent of the population according to different sources), the best strategy is often to leave some flexibility in whether to reveal or conceal that identity.

Markers of Christian religious identity have included items of clothing, names, tattooes or crosses, language elements, jewelry, and pictures of holy symbols. As early as Fatimid and Ayyubid Egypt (A.D. 969–1250), manuscripts indicate that the same rules of feminine modesty applied to Jewish, Muslim, and, it is believed, Coptic women. In public the face had to be veiled, the head covered, and the body enveloped in commodious wraps (Stillman 1976:582). Lane (1954, orig. 1860) writes that the dress of the Christian Copts was fairly similar to the Muslims during the second quarter of the nineteenth century when he visited Cairo. The main difference was that the proper turban of the Christian male was of black,[6] blue, greyish, or light brown color. The Muslim elite male wore a red tarboosh wrapped in a white, often figured shawl to form a turban. Lower-class Muslim men wore white, red, or yellow shawls wrapped around the tarboosh. According to Lane, Copts generally chose dull colors—often black— for their garments. In towns they were careful to wear these distinguishing features but in villages many wore white or red turbans like the Muslims.

Coptic women veiled their faces in public and in their homes when any strange men were present. Unmarried and lower-class women wore white veils and most respectable married women black veils, though many also wore white ones in imitation of Muslims (Lane 1954, orig. 1860: 537). From these reports of Lane and from earlier evidence, it is clear that covering has not been restricted exclusively to Muslims in Egypt, and indeed today, though Christian girls would never adopt Islamic fundamentalist dress, many in the middle classes feel comfortable covering their hair with scarves.

The early evidence above suggests also that modesty garments and the custom of veiling were not newly introduced into Egypt at the time of the Ottoman Empire, as many suggest. The Ottomans most certainly introduced new modesty styles which they, as the controlling authority of the Muslim world of the time, had elaborated into a complicated set of customary dress practices.

By the early 20th century, Ayrout was reporting that the turban of the better off or more pious peasant, for special occasions, consisted of white or brown cloth wound around a cap. Though he attributed this turban to Muslim influence, he noted that Christian peasants wore it equally as much as Muslims (Ayrout 1963; orig. 1938 in French:70). In the space of a century, from the time of Lane's observations to those of Ayrout, distinctions in dress based on religion have nar-

6. Lane says that in A.D. 849–50 the Caliph al-Muttawekkil ordered the Copts to wear honey-colored cloaks. Caliph al-Hakkim in the late tenth century imposed the black turban on Christians. Because the Egyptian caliphs wore white, black was considered the most degrading hue (1954, orig. 1860:555–56).

rowed. In present-day Egypt there are no longer differences in the headdress of ordinary men. Religious leaders of the two communities maintain distinctive turbans and garb, but the lay community has largely reconciled their differences. In the first half of the twentieth century, Christian women of the lower classes tended to wear shawls as head coverings, and to some extent that practice is still continued, although enough Muslims now adopt the head shawl so that even this style is no longer a distinctive marker of Christianity.

During the Ottoman rule in Egypt, it was often disadvantageous to be recognized as a Christian, nor was it easy to blend fully into what was increasingly becoming the Muslim community of Egypt. The Turkish millet system of governing which permitted religious groups to retain their own communities, personal-status legal codes, and their own community leaders, served further to separate religious communities. Non-Muslims were subjected to special taxes, labor quotas for public projects, and other discriminatory acts.

Under British occupation, Coptic Christians expanded some of the economic positions they had held under Muhammad Ali's enlightened reign in the first half of the nineteenth century: customs, government finance departments, tax collection, and business. The Christians symbolized their special relationship with the British by adopting many English personal names for their children, and by being the first Egyptians to accept some of their foreign practices. It was Coptic young women, for example, who were the first to work in public unsegregated employment such as office jobs and to seek extended education. They were also some of the first in the elite classes who took the opportunity (in the name of greater sophistication) to dress in western clothes and move more freely in Egyptian society.[7]

After the Revolution of 1952, with the emerging Islamic character of the government,[8] Christians ceased to feel that a high religious profile was an advantage. At the same time, for political reasons they were anxious to demonstrate the significant numbers of Christian members in the Egyptian Christian community. After the Revolution, Christian families Arabicized the names of their children, choosing ones that were not immediately identifiable as either Muslim or Christian. If the names were taken from the Bible, they were rendered in their Arabic rather than their English form. Father's names or family names, however, often remained unmistakably Christian.

There are several present-day markers of Christianity. Older lower-class women

7. Just the opposite was and is still true in the lower classes, where Christian women are more likely than their Muslim neighbors to stay at home and not seek outside employment.
8. Both Christian and Muslims were involved in the politics of the Revolution, but according to Christians the character of the government rapidly took on Islamic hues. To be fair, the favored position of the Christians in some areas of government service under the British needed redress by a greater employment of Muslims.

frequently have crosses tattooed on their chins to mark indelibly their religious identity. Some said the practice was established to prevent Christians from renouncing their religion, an insurance policy taken out by parents on their children's behavior. Now the custom is to discreetly tattoo the inside of the wrist with a tiny cross. The cross may be hidden by a sleeve or revealed if the hands are arranged properly. Young women of all classes may wear gold crosses, or medallions of the Virgin on chains around their necks; the jewelry may be tucked inside clothing or left to hang outside so it is visible.

The language of Christians is generally free of Muslim expressions like *wallah* (by God), or *wa nabbi* (by the Prophet). A Christian, however, can identify his allegiance by calling on the cross or the Virgin Mary, if it becomes advantageous, as in negotiating a sales with a Christian shopkeeper or asking a favor from a Christian stranger.

In dress, the differences are so subtle and complex that they often must be judged in context. In a district of Cairo known for its numbers of Delta immigrant residents, who are mostly Muslims, a woman seen in a dress typical of Middle Upper Egypt is likely to be a Christian, since a high percentage of the residents coming from those areas are Christians. Lower-class women who wear the melaya liff covering are usually Muslim. Christians say Muslim women look fatter and sleeker, wear more jewelry, dress better, and generally look more prosperous than Christian women of the lower classes. This they say is because Muslim women work harder at being better wives out of fear that if they are not their husbands may divorce them.[9]

Lower-class women are more likely to signal their religious identity than middle- or upper-class Christians, who use little besides their names and incidental pieces of jewelry to make their religious identity known. These higher classes also are less apt to live any more in areas of the city that are identifiably sectarian. During this century areas of the city that were once segregated by sectarian or ethnic criteria have increasingly become identified with economic classes.

The major exception to the general decline in gross distinguishing religious markers in dress is, of course, the increasing use of the fundamentalist zey islami dress which stands out as a clear marker of religious identity. By definition, the dress sets Muslims off from other religious denominations who have no reason to wear the outfit. Fundamentalist dress just as explicitly marks off Muslims of certain persuasions from those who hold more liberal interpretations of Islam.

Christians are put at a disadvantage by this dress, since it makes it impossible for them to hide behind the ambiguities of their markers. They can either hope to remain anonymous among those Muslims who do not wear the fundamentalist dress, or they can play the same game and resort to a clearer marking

---

9. Divorce is almost impossible for Christians in Egypt, while for Muslim men it is little more than a matter of complying with the proper procedures.

of their own identities. As has happened frequently in the history of Christianity in Egypt, there is a resurgence of their religious fervor when Christians feel in some way threatened. People report that the Muslim fundamentalist dress has prompted young Christians to wear their gold crosses more prominently. However, rumors run through the Christian community about crosses being torn from the necks of their wearers by vandals and by religious fanatics, which probably keeps down the numbers wearing crosses. Other young Christian women, however, in an effort to appear less noticeable, have started wearing head scarves with their school uniforms like their Muslim school mates, and see no incompatibility with their religious beliefs in this action.

In areas of Egypt which are uniformly one religion or another there is little need for explicit markers of religious faith. In others, where villages may be alternatingly Muslim and Christian, or where the villages themselves may have subgroups composed of people from the two religions, markers may at one time have assumed greater importance. When a dress marker identifies a religious difference it is difficult to give it up, or to accept a contrasting marker that belongs to the opposing group. Consequently, unless conditions change drastically or another value supercedes religion, dress markers that identify these identities maintain a remarkable stability. This was particularly true for areas in and around Assyut,[10] where pockets of Christians and Muslims were said to have distinguished their communities by wearing waisted and yoked dresses respectively until recently. I could find no clearcut differences along confessional lines any more, though there was an interesting alternation of yoked and waisted styles seen in consecutive villages near Assyut until recently, though no longer based on religious allegiances (see comments on the Shargawi dress of Upper Egyptian Saidis for a possible explanation of this yoked Assyuti village dress).

Markers of religious identity in Egypt are often subtle and complex. Markers which in some contexts symbolize religious allegiance in others signify an overlay of other identities that range from regional to community attachments, and from economic to ethnic distinctions. A person's readiness to identify his or her religious allegiance may depend on social class, the extent to which that membership aids long- or short-term personal goals, and the way the individual feels about his or her own religion and neighboring religious groups.

10. Beni Suef is another area like Assyut where some Egyptians said that Muslims and Christians distinguish themselves by waisted or yoked dresses. I myself have not found that distinction marked in such a way, though perhaps in the past some sort of differentiation along religious lines was clearer.

8

The Dialectic of Dress in Space and Time

"He that is cloaked in what belongs to another is naked"—Arab proverb

THE AUTOBIOGRAPHICAL MOVIE "Alexandria Why?" is set during World War II up to the time of the Egyptian Revolution. Its director, Yusef Shahiin, brilliantly uses the symbols of dress to set the scenes of his complicated plot, instantaneously and in some cases provocatively. Soldiers of course appear in the appropriate uniforms of their countries and their services. Men wear fezes, officers' caps, berets, turbans, and brimmed hats, depending on which elements they portray. Egyptians, marked as British stooges, wear white uniforms and that vestige of foreign imperialism, the Turkish fez. Sadat wears a fez (the audience draws its own conclusions); Nasser does not. A Nubian servant wears an outsized traditional turban. A fisherman with his baggy pants transports the viewer immediately to the salt-water marshes near Alexandria. A regal figure representing the queen comes to watch a school play, wears a Turkish pill-box hat with white veils surrounding her face. Hassan al-Banna, the head of the Muslim Brotherhood, is gowned in an appropriate sheikh's dress. A prosperous Jewish merchant is shown in elegant western style clothes. Servants sit on the floor around a kerosene cooker, a mass of black veils and modesty coverings. A baladi lower-class girl wears a black melaya and scarf but inappropriately shows her bare arms.

Many of the activities involving clothes are symbolic. The young hero throws off his tie as he returns home from his exclusive British school. His mother and sister endlessly ready his clothes for the next excursion out into the public world. But strangely, the boy's impoverished environment is belied by the variety and expense invested in the women's clothes, a lapse an Egyptian viewer may accept as reflecting the family's and the author's attempt to present a good front in public.

Patterns of dress like linguistic categories reveal important clues about the way members of a society conceive their world. Significant social units each have their identifying markers. If people's conceptions about the units change then the way they symbolize them also changes. The observer unravels the subtle patterns of meaning, as in language, by careful attention to their contextual arrange-

161

ments and rearrangements. Again and again, the significant social values are echoed in the behavior of human beings and in its stylistic elements, as if, time and again, people must reconfirm what they feel is important.

Rather than showing the instability of social systems, dress styles show their inherent stability. Seen across space and time, dress patterns show remarkably regular alternation from one socially determined extreme to another. It is in the dialectic of extremes that variety and continuous connection are discovered.

This chapter highlights themes that may have become lost in the considerable detail in previous chapters. Earlier chapters emphasized the recognizable markers of geographic location and community identity—that is, ecological relationships. Later chapters emphasized personal identities, showing how the symbols of sophistication, wealth, age, religion, and educational level often overlay longer-term community and geographic identities to modify them and sometimes to form novel designs.

This chapter now looks at some examples of grand patterns over space and time, patterns of which people are largely unaware. I am assuming that if there were no social significance to dress, then design elements would appear randomly scattered in time and location. But in Egypt just the contrary is true; there are striking relationships across these dimensions. Just as with the geographic markers, it is the gross features of dress that regularly change at this level of the grand design. It is almost axiomatic that the more subtle the distinctions in dress details, the more subtle the messages being relayed and the closer one approaches the shared understandings of in-groups. On the grand scale, by contrast, it is only the observer with the bird's-eye view—which few have the opportunity of possessing—who sees the patterns emerging.

The length of the spatial and temporal fluctuations between "extreme" dimensions in dress, it seems, may be increased or shortened but not entirely extinguished by external circumstances. Up until now, the major stable patterns of Egypt have been the contrasting styles that we have seen already—the waisted dress and the loose granny dress—and each depends on the contrast of the other for its full impact to come clear. To adopt too many elements of the contrasting pattern is to lower the barriers to the "outsider" social group that pattern marks. It is a choice that looms larger than decisions about dress change alone.

Space and time in the world of symbols, as in the world of physics, are concepts that run the risk of distorting reality when separated too rigorously. The variety in dress events viewed at a moment in time, in spatial distribution, may be no more than a series of temporal progressions arrested in a cross-sectional slice. Similarly, temporal progressions may be impeded or facilitated as much by such spatial considerations as proximity and juxtaposition as they are by conscious human desire for novelty. Still, the exercise of looking at these spatial and temporal dimensions provides a new perspective in the attempt to understand contemporary patterns of dress.

SPATIAL DISTRIBUTIONS

The distribution of dress styles across space reveals much about social organization in Egypt. Unlike the periodicities Kroeber reports for Western dress fashions, styles in Egypt do not vacillate around a single stable ideal pattern which constrains the extremes of variation. In Egypt it is contrasting extremes—of waisted and loose-fitting styles—which are the most stable, providing the backbone of dress patterns down the Nile, and serving as a norm to which social groups outside the Valley's immediate circumference can oppose their own styles.

Nile Valley Patterns

Starting from the Mediterranean coast, zones of waisted and yoked dresses alternate in peasant populations.[1] From Alexandria south sixty or more kilometers (where "sophisticate" styles have not obliterated it) is found the waisted "Alexandria" style[2] with full leg-of-mutton sleeves, cuffed wrists, and calf-length skirts. From below Tanta there is an increasing incidence of yoked styles, first with a deep scooped yoke, and eventually changing before Cairo to a moderately scooped yoke. The style remains strong past Cairo until just north of Beni Suef.

From Beni Suef south, the waisted style becomes even more prominent, especially near the towns of Minya and Assyut, and still among a good proportion of the population in Luxor. Near Beni Suef the dress is ankle-length (influenced by the proximity of the ankle-length yoked dress),[3] but by Minya the dress shortens to just below the knee. Between Luxor and Aswan, yoked styles appear again as the Shargawi dresses of the Upper Egyptian Sa'idis.

An interlocking tension of repulsion—of a need to mark differences—maintains the alternating pattern of waisted and yoked dresses through the Nile Valley, suggesting that despite their differences, the inhabitants of these areas share something that makes of them a coherent whole. They relate to one another as much in their repulsive as in their cohesive tendencies. Despite their differences, folk costumes of the Nile Valley are more similar to one another than they are to the styles of oasis dweller or bedouin. One assumes that as long as the distinctions in dress of the Valley dwellers are maintained, important social

1. These distributions ignore for the moment the use of the black "sophisticate" yoked moda overdress that appears to some degree in all urban areas and even in some rural ones as well.
2. This style has all but disappeared in the sophisticated city of Alexandria and is less common where new areas have been inhabited by workers from other areas of the Delta. Its greatest incidence is found now in small towns of the northern coast and in farming areas northeast of Damenhour.
3. Skirt length in other places sometimes is a function of nearness to towns and the greater modesty needs people feel under such circumstances.

differences remain to be marked. When the differences disappear will be the time when the population has reached a degree of homogenization that no longer sees value in the old distinctions.

The alternation of yoked and waisted styles corresponds roughly with the categories Egyptians themselves use to differentiate peoples of the Valley: North Coast, Delta, Middle Upper Egypt, and Deep Upper Egypt. The categories are conceptual rather than strictly political. For example, by the government definition of its boundaries, Upper Egypt begins in Giza, a suburb of Cairo south and west of the Nile. Conceptually, however, Cairenes do not think of their friends on the west bank of the Nile as any different from themselves. They mark the social boundary of Upper Egypt as south of the influence of Cairo, approximately where the dress change occurs at Beni Suef. North Coast similarly has a different "feel" brought about partly because of a different economy—fig cultivation, sheep-herding, fishing, and port activities. Delta inhabitants of the folk classes are usually field farmers. Middle Upper Egyptians (in sa'id il wastani) are also field farmers, but their conservative nature, a strong Christian minority in their villages, and a reputation for hard-headedness, makes them seem different from the more cosmopolitan and sociable Delta people. And the deep southerners (in sa'id il gawwani)—Nubians and their dark-skinned Sa'idi neighbors, both strongly Muslim groups—are another form of conservative, with communities remote from the activities of the major Egyptian centers of Cairo and Alexandria. These are, of course, generalizations that gloss over similarities and are biased toward the perceptions of Cairenes and others who live in Lower Egypt. Nevertheless, because distinctions in dress remain sharply defined, we can reasonably assume that people themselves feel their social differences, even if they do not express them in just these terms.

The single cord that draws the people of the Valley together is composed of other strands than those that simply mark geographical location. Much that is distinctive in an area is embedded in ethnic, ecological, and religious differences. The differences between Nubian and Sa'idi, between bedouin and peasant, and in the recent past between oasis and valley, still remain important enough for rural people to mark with specific designs.

But how then have these dress styles come to be distributed geographically, and what is the process of their distribution? Modesty garments give the clearest example of how innovations spread. Large cities and towns serve as the entry point for many novel patterns. These patterns may spread either on a country-wide scale as in the melaya liff modesty cloak and the moda overdress which have some incidence even in far-flung areas of Egypt, or they may appear in regional variations, as seen in garments such as the Sohag birda, the Assyut shugga, the Sharqiya and the Boheira melas, the Luxor hubbara and jubba, and the Isna tawb. The germs of the ideas for these regional modesty cloaks did not necessarily originate in the towns where they are found today. Many are probably relics that survive from once more popular and widespread styles coming by way of Cairo or Alexandria, or from even further sources such as Turkey. In the areas where they are found today the garments or their materials have remained available for purchase, and for want of competing styles have become characteristic.

It is through centers of population that ideas germinate, and sift down to the remoter surrounding areas. It is not a uniform diffusion from a single entry point to the surrounding countryside. An idea from Cairo, for example, does not spread like the ripple of a stone dropped in a body of water, uniformly in all directions. Instead it skips from point to point, from Cairo to Alexandria to Benha to Tanta to Damenhour, to Minya to Assyut to Aswan, earliest where the city is most receptive to change.[4] From these regional cities and towns the stone skips to smaller towns and from them to villages, and finally the last ripples move out into the hinterlands in directions determined by trade and other contacts. Somewhere along the line the style may be delayed or rejected or incorporated partially into a prevailing style. The rough wool birda may be nothing more than a local coarser version of the elegant Luxor hubbara, for example. And the Assyut shugga, identical in most details with a hubbara found in remote regions of Syria, may come from a single Ottoman inspiration with only a difference in name now marking them. Similarly the distinctive shugga found in Ghaneyem with its attached skirt is reminiscent of the two-piece skirt and cloak hubbara worn earlier in urban Assyut. Distributions across space may be as much a time-lag phenomenon as a geographical one.

Modes of a people's transport significantly facilitate the distribution of dress styles. The restricted travels of villagers in the past have limited the spread of styles to the influences of nearby towns. Women still travel less than men. The effects of waterways (as seen from the examples of the canal leading to Fayoum and the Rosetta branch of the Nile) in bringing styles deep into the hinterland are still in evidence in the distribution of women's styles. Similarly, caravan routes and sea routes have spread dress elements through oases of the Western desert, and to the North and Red Sea coasts. Recently, archeologists[5] are finding evidence that Hadhrami fishermen lived on the coast of Egypt not so long ago, so it is not surprising to find items of clothing or decorative designs in Egyptian caravan towns similar to those found in the Tihama towns of Yemen. Only gradually are major highways taking over the spread of styles in radiating spokes from central provincial capitals. The influences of Egypt's past are found in unexpected

4. There is some indication that economic activity rates affect receptivity to change. In a city like Aswan in Deep Upper Egypt, for example, where High Dam activity attracts outsiders and increases available opportunities, the rate at which people are drawn to accept the models of dress coming from big urban centers like Cairo tends to accelerate. This is partly due to the growing similarities in their populations.

5. Bell, L., Johnson, Janet H., and Whitcomb, Donald. "The Eastern Desert of Upper Egypt: Routes and Inscriptions." Journal of Near Eastern Studies Vol. 43, No. 1, January 1984.

Deep-yoked granny style of the Central Delta.

places and the changes of modern life are an overlay that never completely erases what went before.

Transitions

What happens at the point of transition, where one pattern changes to another? Though they are the places with the most potential for marking contrasts, these rural communities do not generate new styles. Are transitions orderly or unsystematic? Do they occur like a bolt of lightning — here and then not here — or do they mix and gradually fade? Do they affect the adjacent style or do they remain discrete entities?

Deep-yoked granny dress of
the Central Delta.

There are three main transitional points where dresses change from yoked
to waisted or vice versa along the course of the Nile: across the Damenhour-Tanta
axis; north of Beni Suef; and between Armant and Isna. These are all rural areas.
Nearby towns and cities, like urban centers everywhere in Egypt, are subject to
the varied patterns of local, regional, national, and even foreign influence. Here
it is more profitable to look at dress as a temporal progression—that is, to note
the extent to which certain styles are waxing and waning in popularity. A "purer,"
more unadulterated view of spatial distributions is discerned from observing patterns in rural contexts.

The three main transition points in Egypt are characterized by much greater variety in dress pattern than areas at the center of a style's major geographical area. This variety may take the form of several patterns which exist within a village or between villages.

Damenhour-Tanta-Abu Kabir

Across the large upper section of the Delta a belt of towns connects areas of considerable variety in dress. There are differences in silhouette with the waisted leg-of-mutton sleeve dress vying for popularity with yoked granny dresses, older Boheira embire dresses and modern cloche dresses. Yokes and bodices of these dresses vary a great deal in the extent and type of decorative detail as well as in depth of decolletage, whether visibly showing flesh or filled in with cloth insets. Piping frequently outlines the shape of breasts, collars, and yokes. Sleeves may be straight without cuffs, cuffed and full, or gathered without cuffs.

Unique modesty garments like the melas and the bedla persist in the face of an increasing incidence of the moda granny overdress. One common basic dress has a uniquely deep yoke (see illustration).

Perhaps the greatest variety is found in the very heartland of the Delta, in the vast agricultural areas of northern Gharbiya and southern Kafr il Sheikh. From Tukh north one finds an increasing incidence of the deep-yoked granny style. After turning off on the road to Kafr il Sheikh, this dress confronts the waisted style of Alexandria penetrating through market towns into remote rural areas of the region.

By Dessouk the majority of the dresses have become waisted, first long as they meet the challenge of the ankle-length granny style and then shorter as one moves north. In the reclaimed land areas near Metobis, one begins to see even the sirwaal baggy pants of the north coast fisherman worn now on the peasant farmers. In the bigger towns of the area the wrap style melas mingles with the myriad influences found in any large urban area. The variety in the dress of Kafr il Sheikh can partly be laid to the multiple origins of the residents who came in the 1950s to work the reclaimed areas. Otherwise there is little evidence of a greater sophistication in life style or material possessions to explain the variety.

North of Beni Suef

Within a radius of about twenty kilometers north and south of the point where a secondary road connects Fayoum with the main north-south highway of Egypt that borders the Nile, a virtual battle of the granny dress and the waisted dress is waged. The granny dress wins to the north and the waisted dress to the south. The latter emerges in an ankle-length version that shortens quickly so that by Minya, one finds the more common just-below-the-knee length.

Along the forty-kilometer stretch of highway, women in one village may wear mainly granny dresses and in the next, mainly waisted, or there may be strong incidence of both styles in the same village. Tarha veils and shawls may be worn with both styles or in a single village the incidence of one or the other may be stronger. Decorative detail on the bodices and yokes of dresses varies in the same way.

Common in the waisted style is a fitted band around the abdomen to below the breasts, and elaborate tucks and decorative additions on the upper bodice that emphasize the size of the breasts. The decorative details give the effect of a short bolero style jacket covering the upper body with inset piece at the neck-line seeming to be part of a dress appearing underneath. Because of the variety and beauty of costumes in the area, the region between the barrages north of Cairo and as far south as Beni Suef is the best place to observe a range of Egyptian costumes.

Armant to Isna

Luxor used to identify more strongly with Middle Upper Egypt because of its large Christian community. But now with the out-migration of many of the old Christian families to urban centers like Cairo, and the in-migration of Nubians for work in the tourist trade, Luxor becomes the first town where one sees the blending of Middle and Deep Upper Egyptian styles. It is in the countryside south of Luxor, however, that the instability of patterns is clearest. South of Luxor the use of modesty garments in addition to the shawl increases significantly.

Just before Armant, waisted dresses of calf-length begin to mix with longer ankle-length waisted dresses. The hubbara of Luxor begins to disappear and in its place is seen the thawb, the black modesty garment like a man's galabiya. A birda-like shawl of large dimensions competes with tarha and standard shawls as head covering. As one moves south, the tawb becomes more prominent and its incidence becomes mixed with the transparent jirjara of the Nubian. The shawls also begin to change from black to vivid colors of red, orange, green, and blue.

In Isna one sees the whole range of the identifiably Upper Egyptian garments: the shugga, the hubbara, the jubba, the ferka, the nishra, and the birda. Slowly after Idfu, the yoked Sa'idi shargawi dress and the Nubian jirjara stabilize into their consistent stance as contrasting styles marking two communities. Both are yoked, making a clear contrast with the Middle Upper Egyptian dress, but both are also different enough so that one is not easily confused with the other.

In this same area from Armant to a little further south at Idfu, many of the peasant men work wearing a black calf-length skirt with black vest and long-sleeve black undershirt. Others wear the standard galabiya.

People in these transitional areas can afford to be more eclectic in their choices, and are less likely in some cases to assign consistent meanings to styles they select, because community norms are not so narrowly fixed. For example, a woman from the town of Aiyat (north of Beni Suef) commented that she wore waisted or yoked dresses as she pleased, and added that heavier women would probably be more likely to wear yoked dresses because they were more commodious and therefore more comfortable. In this area of transition, if there are no significant geographical or community meanings to convey, people take the opportunity to select what is pleasing to them, within the limits of what they consider appropriate to their rank, personal status, and age. The presentation of self is given freer play within the possibilities offered by a less invariable and structured system of meanings in dress. It would be interesting to know if people within these communities themselves, in other activities of their lives, reveal more individuality and creativity.

Consciously, people are not always aware of marking distinctions or of their styles creating patterned distributions in space. A Delta woman, at first contact, is more likely to note the "archaic" look of an Upper Egyptian dress, or the Upper Egyptian to castigate the "immorality" of Delta women in their "sophisticate" styles. Some markers may have passed through periods of conscious design that have left their legacy on styles. For example, the waisted dress of the Christian and the yoked dress of the Muslim may have begun as styles that marked religious communities in certain areas of Egypt, but now the markers are no longer cogent and the boundaries have blurred. When they meet, people react to certain symbols in one another's dress as individuals, as community members, and as participants in a general pattern of symbolic statements across space and time, without sometimes being fully aware of their participation in these exchanges.

TEMPORAL DISTRIBUTIONS

Notions of modesty—of how much of the body should be covered—serve as a good example of how dress norms vary historically as well as contemporaneously. The norm does not always move to lighter and more revealing coverings. Nubia is a case in point, where acceptable dress for women ranged from almost complete nakedness at the end of the eighteenth century to a rough cloth covering by the middle of the nineteenth century to the current jirjara and shawl, one of the most conservative covers. As mediators between Arab and African cultures, Nubians have sometimes felt ambivalent about their attachment to one or the other. Much of the change in their dress style in the last two centuries probably represents a deepening involvement of Egyptian Nubians both economically and psychologically in more conservative mainstream Egyptian life. The new transparent jirjara covering the foreign clothes of the educated Nubian girl is one step further in the melding of Nubian and middle class urban Egyptian mainstream styles. For the Nubian, the final synchronization with the conservative and liberal swings of middle-class Egyptian dress occurs with the adoption of fundamentalist styles, which for them, as conservative Muslims, is within the range of viable choice.

The Nubian example is repeated in the conservative-liberal-conservative swings of other Egyptian subgroups. At the turn of the nineteenth century, artists accompanying the Napoleonic expedition depicted Egyptian women wearing half-veils and dark, light-weight dresses with deep cut-out necklines that exposed the cleavage of their breasts. Men of the working classes wore loosely sashed gowns reaching to a little below the knee. Elite men wore rich robes that extended to their ankles. Elite women, too, wore highly decorated, many-layered outfits that reached to the ground. By the mid-nineteenth century urban upper-class women were wearing an even more ponderous bulk of multi-layered garments that not only completely covered the body but largely obscured the basic human shape. When appearing in public, yet another large silk cloak (the hubbara) and a face veil was added to the bulk.

Over the decades, with the advent of general education and the "rationalization" of women's minds that is credited with greater internalized as opposed to externalized enforcement of social controls, modesty became a function of a person's compliance with subgroup definitions of appropriateness. Elite and middle-class styles emulated the foreign dress models that came to symbolize sophistication and an educated status—values these classes came to admire. The brevity of these styles when compared with previous fashions was justified in terms of the greater self-control expected of the educated, and by the greater leeway accepted for the behavior of the powerful. By the late 1960s many of these groups were wearing the sleeveless, abbreviated mini-skirt style then popular in the Western world. The dress of actresses appearing in Egyptian movies of the time appears scandalous when viewed from the perspective of contemporary middle-class conservatives now wearing fundamentalist dress.

Early nineteenth-century elite styles were lost completely except for those styles taken over by the lower classes who could afford them. The inhabitants of large cities are primarily responsible for many of the changes in folk styles. Frequently the urban lower classes mediate the innovations between higher classes and folk classes of the countryside. The lower classes rarely adopt an elite costume fully since to do so would be presumption; rather they take elements that fit their sense of appropriateness. Often the modesty garment suits this criterion since it does not alter the basic dress that is worn for everyday occasions, but can be used for formal events when an element of presumption is not unfitting. However, when a style becomes common to the lower classes, elites feel impelled to find a new style for themselves, in order to keep crystal clear the distinctions between the classes. In the following example from Assyut we see the dynamics of this process.

During the early years of the century, the higher classes wore loose or waisted floor-length dresses with a shugga cape that was folded double over the head and shoulders, but falling in a single layer from there to the floor. A belt gathered the single layer at the waist. By about the third decade of the century, this form of shugga was common in the traditional quarters of Assyut, and eventually spread in the abbreviated form of a cloak to prosperous villagers in towns near Assyut. Associated with prosperity, the garment is still popular today.

Peasants who use the garment usually wear a waisted dress with sometimes a ruffled train underneath and largely concealed by it. Meanwhile, more sophisticated townspeople had taken up the two piece hubbara with elasticized long skirt (da'ira) and a shawl-like piece that extends from center forehead, over the head and to the waist. Ties over the ears which are bound behind the head keep the top part of the hubbara in place. This type of hubbara no longer exists in Egypt; the contemporary hubbara is a single piece of rectangular cloth. It is reported that underdresses were selected on the basis of preferred style and comfort (usually full ankle-length dresses for the corpulent and older women, and waisted ankle-length styles for the young and shapely). With the enveloping cloaks, the underdresses, in any case, were barely visible on excursions out into public, and therefore were not essential in conveying critical information.

Next, urban educated and elite classes adopted the *burneeta* (foreign style hat) and the *balto,* a long coat-style of heavy material, with fitted waists, lapels, and full-length buttoning. It was, in effect, a coat to be worn over a dress that was also foreign-inspired. Another style of the times was the *tailleur* (a two piece suit), worn sometimes under the shugga cloak or sometimes alone without a modesty garment. One elderly Assyuti woman noted that her husband told her to remove the head scarf and wear foreign clothes like the tailleur and the balto because he worked with foreigners and did not want her to give them an impression of backwardness.

Now Assyutis with any degree of education adopt foreign dress or, if they are Muslim, the other alternative for the educated, Islamic dress. Most peasants of the region still wear yoked or waisted dresses, some people say as a relic of days when the differences marked religious communities. Now in some villages south of Assyut the close resemblance of women's dress with the Boheira embire style suggests a Delta origin to some yoked dresses.

Recently several rural women from near Assyut met in the house of a Cairene cousin for a funeral. The visiting country cousins wore waisted, black, square-necked, ankle-length dresses with fitted bodices and narrow cuffed sleeves, black, small head scarves, and a tarha wrapped around the head. The Cairo cousin's dress contained all the same decorative elements as that of the rural women, but her dress was just below knee-length, and she wore no tarha over her head scarf. She wears this same outfit both inside and outside of her house.

Her explanation for the difference was that in the city one sees all kinds of styles accepted by the people, and with a hint of condescension, added that people in the cities are more modern. Long-term residence in the city is likely to have the effect of a greater casualness in dress. Short excursions to the city by rural women have the opposite effect, and cause much more circumspection about dress, in particular with attention to covering. These country cousins all wore heavy shawls when they descended into the street.

In Assyut, changes in dress styles in the twentieth century for the elites and the middle classes have primarily involved a move from heavy concealment with commodious modesty garments to dress of foreign inspiration that gradually dropped specialized modesty apparel. Now with the use of the fundamentalist dress by some, the trend has reversed to a greater concentration on the modesty aspects of dress. Even those who wear foreign dress are careful to conceal their arms, lengthen their skirts, and sometimes to wear head scarves.

For the rural lower classes, living near Assyut, there is a modified lag effect, only partly related to the dress of the higher urban classes. The lower classes earlier were not so much concerned with concealment. It was the rich among them that took up with enthusiasm the elaborate modesty cloaks of urbanites, and then mainly as a way of showing their higher economic status. If heavier covering became the norm for country elites, lighter covering became more fashionable for those who migrated to cities like Cairo. Even now, each year many young married women of the lower urban classes wear shorter sleeves, lighter materials, and fewer head coverings when they go about their daily tasks inside and outside of their homes. The ubiquitous formal modesty garment, the moda yoked overdress, as an exception to this tendency, shows the variety in acceptable dress one finds now. The practical advantages of the moda dress (as well as its acceptance as fashion) may weigh as heavily as its modesty functions. It covers a shabby basic dress, is comfortable for all types of figure, and leaves the hands free for all manner of activity. Thus, the temporal sequence of tendencies to reveal and conceal the physical body may not run exactly parallel in the various social classes.

Assyut in some respects is unique as a result of the important roles American missionaries played in the educational institutions of the town. Foreigners demonstrated how one could be both "uncovered" and also modest and respectable at the same time. Similar changes took place in dress in other parts of urban Egypt at about the same time, however, either as the result of foreign models or from indigenous elites who in the temper of the times were turning for inspiration outside the boundaries of the country.

In the three examples of Nubia, the urban centers of Egypt, and the specific case of Assyut, we see roughly outlined (among other changes) a community's redefinition of what parts of the body are considered appropriate to reveal and what to conceal. Quite often the changes appear to involve vacillation between greater cover and lighter cover and back again to heavy cover. One way to look at these periodicities is to see them as the natural outcome of the victory and defeat of the tensions between extremes in dress dimensions. The more the style adopts the characteristics of one extreme, the stronger the tension develops to right the balance and move back toward a contrasting style. The attraction of the opposing extreme in such moments becomes stronger and wins out for a time until that attraction fades and the opposite contrast becomes more appealing again.

This way of conceiving the problem may be no more than to say that people crave a certain amount of variety in their lives. Within the momentary parameters of choice, they seek first one identifiable contrast in their dress and then another. Human thought processes that define qualities in terms of oppositions — of large and small, fat and thin — have always inherent in them that ghostlike trace of what was given up to achieve a particular reality. Adding to this natural way of conceiving the world are the committed groups seeking, for their own reasons, visible and distinctive differences: younger generations wanting styles different from their parents; social, economic, religious, and ethnic groups all striving for uniqueness in their symbolic representation; elites, whose very leadership depends on acting as trend setters; and finally individuals looking for small modifications that express their own special identities.

Historically, the impetus for much of the novelty in dress has come from the higher social classes, not always simply as a whim for variety. One scholar sees the main function of the veil in earlier periods of Egypt's history as a means of differentiating the social classes (Abu Zahra 1970:1086). The veil set the elites apart when it was commonly worn by those classes, as much as when, in the 1920s under the leadership of Hoda Sharawi they removed it. Only the socially secure at the time could afford such daring. Seen from a similar class perspective, the donning of Islamic dress marks the newly growing middle class, and the fashion trend setters are people who were sensitive to the needs of that class for social definition. The trend to Islamic dress also fits the dialectic model as a reactive phase to the brevity of foreign dress, both in the specific sense because it is antithetical to orthodox religious interpretations of modesty, and in the general sense, as foreign and alien to Islamic cultural inspiration.[6]

Conservativism, as so many values, tends to be relative, requiring an opposing value to define it. Upper Egypt is usually considered much more conservative than the Delta regions. Yet the knee-length waisted styles of many Upper Egyptians appear less conservative by anyone's measures, when contrasted with

---

6. One writer says, "The monkey-like imitation by our youngsters, both boys and girls, of all that comes from the West is a bad thing which they should refrain from. . . . The tight jeans adapted to "the daughter of Uncle Sam" will never suit an Egyptian girl. They expose more than they hide. . . . That is life. We have to watch, discern and look before we leap" (Mai Shaheen, in *Al-Akhbar,* translation from the *Egyptian Gazette,* December 15, 1980).

the shape-concealing granny styles of women from the Delta. Are these Upper Egyptian areas, by reason of their remoteness, to be considered a more resistant vestige of briefer styles, that through a time lag have not yet met the influence of the modern swing to conservativism? The "conservative" black moda granny overdress is after all a style still only about fifteen or twenty years old and spreading more quickly in the areas close to Cairo. Or has the briefer style become so strongly equated with geographical markers which still retain some cogency that people of Upper Egypt are reluctant to adopt too quickly the symbols of Delta and urban Cairenes? The middle-class adoption of dress symbols that are either foreign or universally Islamic and have no specific local meaning may facilitate their ease of general acceptance. The symbols are geographically neutral, focusing on the value of education that everyone can accept.

The growing value placed on educational status was in many ways a momentous event in Egyptian history. It is the most recent major value to generate a consensus overriding the significance of previous social markers. It has had, and will have in the future, important implications in terms of social mobility, equality, and homogenization of the Egyptian population. Until recently, Egyptians have been fairly rigidly contained in the social status of their birth, with few avenues of escape into more valued economic and occupational categories. The rush to the adoption of foreign dress is a visible reminder of the unleashed aspirations of the lower classes that now have some hope of success. Within this changed situation is an accumulation of events, of better transportation, of access to better service opportunities, of a drawing together of all parts of Egypt into more frequent communication, either direct, or relayed through the public media. The homogenization of the population like the homogenization of dress is far from complete. Women, for example, have not as yet been offered the same exposure to these events as men, and as a result, their folk styles, as their life styles, still serve to maintain viable alternative sets of local values. Other elements of the population are similarly circumscribed by their environments in ways that prevent them from taking full advantage of the opportunities that are open for larger numbers of Egyptians today.

The values of place and community erode quickly when put in competition with urban middle-class values that carry with them the promise of better opportunities. When these values become widespread and mainstream, the interplay of the symbolic dialectic is reduced in spatial and temporal terms. Then, as in Kroeber's example of Western fashions, the concern becomes whether a skirt is raised or lowered a few inches over time, and variations of style throughout the country tend to be reduced to time-lag phenomena, as a fashion moves slowly out to the countryside from the single generating source of most importance — the urban center. At that point, the main measure of variation is reduced to an urban-rural, modern-old fashioned distinction that renders secondary the range of markers that were significant before. In Egypt, we have seen the extent to which distinctive elements in male dress have already been reduced by the pressure of these forces.

The second major change is the central role performed by the middle classes in determining the styles for the broad range of Egyptians, for the lower classes who seek the rewards of upward mobility, as well as for elites, whose conservative stance binds them automatically to mainstream styles. At present one of these fashions is the new fundamentalist dress. Although Egypt as yet has not completed this trend, its dress patterns indicate that it is well on the way toward homogenization in the values of its people.

The city of Port Said on the northern coast of Egypt exemplifies this more than any other city of the country. The special characteristics of Port Said are the high educational level of its population, an economy based to considerable extent on commercial free-zone import activities, and a sparsely populated hinterland with little impact on urban values and styles. Some of the residents who work in the Suez Canal Authority assemble from other parts of Egypt and thus reside far from the influence of other local values. Port Said has a large Christian minority and a number of Greek and Italian permanent residents. Access to foreign-made clothing is easy and cheap because of the tax-free status of the city.

The majority of the residents of Port Said wear foreign clothes, with blue jeans by far the most prominent style among young people. What is different from the jean-wearing populations of Cairo is the broader range of social classes that wear them in Port Said. Construction workers, agricultural laborers, shoe-shine boys, and vegetable vendors all wear jeans in the city, and some farmers even wear them to work in the fields outside of the city. Jeans have been demoted from every-day "dress-up" clothes to actual every-day work clothes, presentable almost everywhere. It is the only area in Egypt (except on government agricultural projects sometimes) where foreign styles are worn by farmers. Only rarely in Port Said is folk dress visible, and then clearly being worn by visitors from villages outside the city. As in Cairo, fundamentalist dress is frequently observed among young middle-class urban women and the trend is increasing.

Port Said's uniformity of dress style may be considered, on the one hand, as an ultimate stage in a progression of styles tending toward the standardization of dress in all Egypt—a homing in on certain central values that obscure the importance of previously held values. On the other, Port Said's unique configuration of characteristics, largely a result of a particular geographical location, may make of it a momentary focus of certain contemporary tendencies that after a while will lose their temporary strength. In that case it is possible that Port Said, without any strong identities of its own, will remain peripheral in its dress styles to larger cities like Cairo and Alexandria. At the moment, Port Said is in a position to intensify the styles coming out of those cities, but it is not, by the nature of its circumstances, in a position where one would expect it to take the lead in creating new styles, unless those styles were imported ones.

What, one may ask, becomes the valued symbol after the opportunities of education become so widespread that they no longer require significant markers? Until new categories of value replace education and develop correlates in dress, we cannot know. Already "foreign-ness" is losing its original cogency and no longer calls the game plays of dress for certain groups so forcefully. Will Islamic dress provide the unmistakable stamp of indigenous origins that people seek today? Can it be that piety, as marked in progressive stages of Islamic dress, and the greater incidence of religious symbols in Christians' jewelry, will become the superceding value in the next few years, breaking down the earlier consensus built around education? Or will the role of fundamentalist dress as marker of social class diminish and be replaced with other class markers, demonstrating its intrinsic nature as a social rather than religious symbol? Are there styles in the offing that, better than the variety in foreign dress, serve the corporate interests of Egyptian culture, permitting individuals to mark their essential oneness with their fundamental social groups? The Islamic fundamentalist dress is one such possibility but there may be other alternatives in the future.

At present, to the extent to which local values dictate a person's priorities, dress styles retain distinctive markers of geographic place and local community. The extent to which Egyptians of all localities merge their values in national or wider urban standards determines how many people don the homogenized dress styles of the urban "folk sophisticate" or the educated middle class. The extent to which they identify their values with the West or the countries of the Gulf and Saudi Arabia is the extent to which they allow foreign influence to set the content of their fashion trends. The implications go far beyond dress to what in broader terms constitutes social value. Dress styles help to consolidate changes in social perspective by permanently marking them; they do not, in themselves, create changes in outlook. The dialectic of what to reveal and what to conceal is resolved at each moment and in each place by individual interpretations of social principles of appropriateness—principles that the social group in its own struggle with the dialectic has momentarily resolved to its own satisfaction.

Bibliography

Abu-Zahra, N.M. 1970. "On the Modesty of Women in Arab Muslim Villages—A Reply." *American Anthropologist* 72, pp. 1079–87.

Ayrout, H.H. 1963 (1945 edition, orig. 1938 in French). *The Egyptian Peasant.* Boston: Beacon Press.

Blackman, W.S. 1968. *The Fellahen of Upper Egypt.* Totowa, N.J.: Biblio Distributers.

Bull, D. and D. Lorimer. 1979. *Up the Nile: A Photographic Excursion: Egypt 1839–1898.* New York: Clarkson N. Potter.

Evans, Mary. 1950 revised. *Costume Through the Ages.* Philadelphia: Lippincott.

Fahmy, H. 1979. "Changing Women in a Changing Society: The Study of Emergent Consciousness of Young Women in the City of Akhmiim in Upper Egypt." In *Child Development in Egypt,* ed. N.V. Ciaccio, Cairo Papers in Social Science, Volume 3, Monograph 2, December. Cairo: American University in Cairo Press.

Fakhouri, H. 1972. *Kafr el-Elow: An Egyptian Village in Transition.* New York: Holt, Rinehart and Winston.

Fakhry, A. 1973. *The Oases of Egypt, Volume I: Siwa Oasis.* Cairo: American University in Cairo Press.

———. 1974. *The Oases of Egypt, Volume II: Bahriyah and Farafra Oases.* Cairo: American University in Cairo Press.

Fernea, R.A. and G. Gerster. 1973. *Nubians in Egypt.* Austin: University of Texas Press.

Gordon, L.D. 1969 (orig. 1865). *Letters from Egypt (1862–1869).* London: Routledge and Kegan Paul.

Haddad, Yvonne Y. 1982. "The Case of the Feminist Movement," in *Contemporary Islam and the Challenge of History.* Albany, N.Y.: SUNY Press.

Harris, M. 1973. "What Goes Up, May Stay Up." In *Natural History* 72, no. 1, pp. 18–25.

Ibrahim, Barbara. 1980. "Social Change and the Industrial Experience: Women as Production Workers in Urban Egypt." Ph.D. dissertation, Indiana University, p. 84.

Kennedy, John G. 1977. *Struggle for Change in a Nubian Community: An Individual in Society and History.* Los Angeles: University of California, Mayfield Publishing Company.

Khuri, F. 1975. *From Village to Suburb: Order and Change in Greater Beirut.* Chicago: University of Chicago Press.

Kroeber, A.L. 1919. "On the Principle of Order in Civilization as Exemplified by Changes in Fashion." In *American Anthropologist,* N.S. 21, pp. 235–263.

Lane, E.W. 1954 (orig. 1860). *Manners and Customs of the Modern Egyptians.* London: J.M. Dent and Sons, Ltd.

Makhlouf, Carla. 1979. *Changing Veils: Women and Modernization in North Yemen.* Austin: University of Texas Press.

Picken, Mary B. 1973 (orig. 1939). *The Fashion Dictionary.* New York: Funk and Wagnalls.

Richardson, J. and A. Kroeber. 1940. "Three Centuries of Women's Dress Fashions: A Quantitative Analysis." In *Anthropological Records* 5, no. 2, pp. 111–54.

Ross, H.C. 1980. "Fashion in the Sand." In *Aramco World* November–December.

Stillman, Y.A. 1976. "The Importance of the Cairo Geniza Manuscripts for the History of Medieval Female Attire." In *International Journal of Middle East Studies* 7, 1976: 579–589.

Webster, Sheila K. 1984. "Harim and Hijab: Seclusive and Exclusive Aspects of Traditional Muslim Dwelling and Dress." In *Women's Studies Int. Forum* 7, no. 4, pp. 254–57.

Wilcox, R. Turner. 1969. *The Dictionary of Costume.* New York: Charles Scribner's Sons.

Williams, John A. 1980. "Veiling in Egypt as a Political and Social Phenomenon." In Esposito, ed. *Islam and Development.* Syracuse, New York: Syracuse University Press.

Wingate, Isabel B. 1979, sixth ed. *Fairchild's Dictionary of Textiles.* New York: Fairchild Publications.

Index

A-line dress silhouette. *See* dress locations: Isna, Siwa; Dress: patterns

Abaya (cloak). *See* Dress: men's

Abu Ruwwash, 44–46

Agal (head rope). *See* Dress: men's

"Alexandria" dress. *See* Dress: patterns

Allamun, 58, 59, 63

Arish, 86, 90, 91, 94, 96, 97

Assyut, vii, xi, 15, 18, 36, 41, 43, 160, 164, 165, 171–73

Aswan, 47, 48

Awrah (parts of body to be covered), 153. *See also* Modesty: norms

Bahriya, x, 12, 39, 54, 63, 66–70, 76. *See also* Bawiti; Harrah

Baladi, vii, 7, 161. *See also* Dress: folk

Ballot, 1, 2, 60–64

Bawiti, 67, 112

Bayad, 35, 54, 55

Bedla. *See* Dress: patterns

Bedouin, vii, 20, 28, 56, 62, 66, 77–98, 101, 102

Beja, 102

Beni Suef, 18, 53, 54, 160, 164, 168, 170

Benish (robe). *See* Dress: men's

Birda. *See* Modesty garments

Boheira, 8, 26–28, 32, 43, 100, 109, 172

Bonné. *See* Modesty garments

Bortus, 44–46

Cairo, ii, vii, 18, 19, 25, 32, 43, 53, 105, 108, 140, 159, 163, 175, 176

Cap. *See* Dress: men's

Caravan routes: as influence on dress, ix, 39, 42, 53, 66, 67, 72, 74, 75, 96, 102, 165

Children. *See* Dress: children's

Christians
dress of, 157–60
as minority religious group, 156, 158–60, 164
See also Markers of identity

Cities: as source of influence on dress, 34, 92, 104, 140, 165–67, 173–75

Class, social, 104, 106, 117, 123, 159, 160, 176. *See also* Dress; Markers of identity

Cloak. *See* Dress: men's; Modesty garments

Cloche. *See* Dress: patterns

Coast, North, ix, 98

Coast, Red Sea, 101. *See also* Beja

Communities: as source of dress norms, 44, 47, 102, 170

Dakhla, 54, 58–67, 70. *See also* Allamun; Ballot

Delta, viii, ix, 17–34, 43–47, 49, 101, 105, 106, 109, 147, 170, 172, 175. *See also* Abu Ruwwash; Boheira; Bortus; Cairo; Gharbiya; Kalubiya; Menufia; Sharqiya

Dress
and climate, 12
children's, ii, 49, 50, 74, 115, 118, 120, 131–33, 161
Christian, vii, viii, 15, 18, 157, 158, 160, 170

REVEAL AND CONCEAL

was composed in 11-point Digital Compugraphic Garamond and leaded 2 points
by Metricomp;
with display type set in Abbott Old Style
by Rochester Mono/Headliners;
printed by sheet-fed offset on 50-pound, acid free Warren's Old Style,
Smyth sewn and bound over binder's boards in Holliston Roxite B
by Thomson-Shore, Inc.;
with dust jackets printed in two colors
by Philips Offset Company, Inc.;
and published by

SYRACUSE UNIVERSITY PRESS
SYRACUSE, NEW YORK 13244-5160